PLAYS FROM VAULT 6

FANBOY
Joe Sellman-Leava

FIVE YEARS WITH THE WHITE MAN
Eloka Obi and Saul Boyer

HONOUR-BOUND
Zahra Jassi

HOW WE BEGIN
Elisabeth Lewerenz

I FUCKED YOU IN MY SPACESHIP
Louis Emmitt-Stern

T0386237

Also Available from Nick Hern Books

PLAYS FROM VAULT 6

FANBOY
Joe Sellman-Leava

FIVE YEARS WITH THE WHITE MAN
Eloka Obi and Saul Boyer

HONOUR-BOUND
Zahra Jassi

HOW WE BEGIN
Elisabeth Lewerenz

I FUCKED YOU IN MY SPACESHIP
Louis Emmitt-Stern

NICK HERN BOOKS
London
www.nickhernbooks.co.uk

A Nick Hern Book

Plays from VAULT 6 first published in Great Britain in 2023 as a paperback original by Nick Hern Books Limited, The Glasshouse, 49a Goldhawk Road, London W12 8QP, in association with VAULT Festival

The authors have asserted their moral rights

Cover artwork by Damien Stanton

Designed and typeset by Nick Hern Books, London
Printed and bound in Great Britain by Mimeo Ltd, Huntingdon, Cambridgeshire PE29 6XX

A CIP catalogue record for this book is available from the British Library

ISBN 978 1 83904 060 3

Contents

Welcome to VAULT Festival

Hoo boy! What does one even begin to write here? I don't know. Better writers than I have articulated the myriad emotions and effects of the last three years. Words seem inadequate. But this is a volume celebrating words and writing and writers so I'm going to give it a red hot go.

It's been rough, hey team? It's been rough for the arts. Even more so for theatre and live performance. Even even more so for fringe and independent theatre. And even even even more so for emerging artists. If anything has been made clear these last few years, it is that there is a dearth of quality and financially sustainable opportunities for early career artists to make work and spaces to make that work in. When those few opportunities are taken away, everyone loses. Artists lose the opportunity to experiment and take risks. Audiences lose the opportunity to engage with exciting and radical work from a multiplicity of voices. And our industry loses the opportunity to grow, progress, be challenged and changed by these voices. It's a long road to recovery with lots of listening and learning required. I really hope we're up for it.

VAULT Festival has not been immune to the decimation of these last years. From the early cancellation in 2020, to deciding not to mount a 2021 Festival, and then the devastating decision to cancel a completely programmed Festival for 2022, this has been a truly difficult time for our artists and our team. Throughout this time it has been made clear to me over and over what a vital part of the live performance ecology VAULT Festival is. How important it is that we are here, providing quality opportunities in the most sustainable way possible for artists and audiences. That we are listening and growing and provoking. Providing space for artists to challenge and disrupt, to ask of an industry on its knees... 'What if?'

The writers included in this, our sixth *Plays from VAULT* anthology, have all used their work to ask 'What if?' These are plays of importance, of playfulness, of risk, of freneticism and pathos and joy and anger and hope. Plays from artists across backgrounds, and styles and forms. I am so very proud of all of them.

These plays represent a mere fraction of the scope of work at VAULT Festival 2023. From stand-up comedy to late-night cabaret, from improvisation to live art and experimental installation, from linear narrative drama to absurdist immersive work, and genres I couldn't even have imagined, VAULT Festival will tear back into the world with a scream. A scream of rage and catharsis. Of fear and hope. A scream of defiance. Our artists, both in this volume and beyond, are here. They are ready. They are fearless. They are disrupting. Because what we did yesterday is not sufficient for tomorrow. And we are up for the challenge.

WE'RE BACK, BABY!!!!

Bec Martin (she/her)
Head of Programming
VAULT Festival 2023

This text went to press before the end of rehearsals and so may differ slightly from the plays as performed.

FANBOY

Joe Sellman-Leava

For Umesh

JOE SELLMAN-LEAVA

Joe grew up in Gloucestershire and Devon. He co-founded Worklight Theatre in Exeter in 2011, with whom he devised and performed several plays, including *How to Start a Riot*. His first solo play, *Labels*, won a Scotsman Fringe First in 2015 and toured the UK and internationally. His second solo show, *Monster*, also toured from 2017, and won VAULT Festival's Show of the Week in 2018. Joe's third solo show, *Fanboy*, had a work-in-progress run at VAULT Festival 2020, where his short, rapid-response piece, commissioned for Extinction Rebellion's *Decolonise: Decarbonise*, also played. He has various screen projects in development, and has written episode scripts for *Pip and Posy* (Magic Light), *The Adventures of Paddington* (Heyday Films) and *Lu and the Bally Bunch* (Lubird Productions). Joe also works as an actor for stage and screen, including *Rain Man* (Bill Kenwright Ltd) and *Great Things Happen at Home* (Brother Brother Film).

Fanboy was first performed as a work-in-progress in 2020 at the Wardrobe Theatre and VAULT Festival. It premiered in 2022 at Pleasance Dome, Edinburgh Festival Fringe, followed by a UK and Ireland tour, a week at Soho Theatre, and then VAULT Festival, London, on 7 March 2023. The cast was as follows:

JOE/OLD JOE	Joe Sellman-Leava
YOUNG JOE	Ethan El-Shater
Director	Yaz Al-Shaater
Technical Designer,	Dylan Howells
Stage Manager & Operator	
Dramaturg	Lauren Mooney
Assistant Director	Hetty Hodgson
Stage Manager & Operator	Alice Winter
(*Soho Theatre/Belltable*)	
Video & Sound Designer	Yaz Al-Shaater
Outside Eyes	Emma Louise-Howell,
	James Rowland,
	Callum Elliott-Archer
Producers	Joe Sellman-Leava
	and Worklight Theatre
Design Consultant	Charlotte Anderson
Poster Image	Ben Borley
Production Shots	Duncan McGylnn
Graphic Designer	Jason Howells
PR (*Edinburgh and tour*)	Chloé Nelkin Consulting
Tour Booker	Maddie Wilson

Acknowledgements

Thank you to Yaz, Dylan, Lauren and Hetty for your creativity, energy and generosity – making this with you was such a privilege; to Alice, for learning 456 cues in no time at all; to James, Emma and Callum for unlocking so much, so joyfully, and to Nemo Martin and Daniel Goldman for your brilliant questions.

Thank you to Jonathan Haldon and Brother Brother for helping make our videos look so cool (and to Yaz, again, for the countless hours of editing!).

Thank you to Arts Council England for making all this possible; to David Byrne for your advice; to Jonny Patton for believing in the show; to everyone at New Diorama Theatre, Pleasance, the Kenton Theatre, Underground Venues, The Tolmen Centre and Exeter Phoenix, for giving us space to play.

Thank you to Frances Arnold for your belief, expertise and tireless work; to Sarah Liisa Wilkinson and everyone at Nick Hern Books; to Lakesha Arie-Angelo and Bec Martin, for each giving this show a home in London.

Thank you to Bríd Doherty, for your endless support (and your world-class flyering!); to my family and friends, for who you are and all you do.

And a very, very special thank you to Ethan El-Shater, for lending us your magic!

J.S-L

Note on Play

This play was originally written to be performed by
Joe Sellman-Leava, a mixed-race man in his early thirties.
In our production, Joe also plays other characters, including:

DAVID ATTENBOROUGH
DAD
OBI
WAYNE
GAIA
DAVID DIMBLEBY
NIGEL FARAGE
DONALD TRUMP
MICHAEL CAINE
EMPEROR PALPATINE

Joe also performs the fan-films, with speed and precision.

The projected HOODED FIGURE (later OLD JOE) is
pre-recorded, also played by Joe, in make-up, to look like
a fifty-year-old version of himself.

The character of YOUNG JOE – an eight-year-old – also
appears via pre-recorded video. He is played, in our production,
by Ethan El-Shater, who looks uncannily like Joe did at that
age. Initially, we should believe it is from an actual home video
the performer is sharing with us.

In these home videos, we also hear the voice of OBI – forties –
again pre-recorded (in our production, by director and video
designer Yaz Al-Shaater).

Finally, there are moments where Joe will speak to the show's
technical operator (in our production, Dylan Howells), who will
occasionally answer back.

House music: 'My Hero' (Foo Fighters), 'Little Red Corvette'
(Prince), 'The Logical Song' (Supertramp), 'I'm Not Your Hero'
(Tegan and Sara), 'Hotel Song' (Regina Spektor), 'Blame it on
my Youth' (Blink-182).

Prologue

Stage-left, a cabinet, holding a nineties-style TV set, a Super
Nintendo, and VHS player, as well as various games,
magazines, books, videos, toys and merchandise. On the top of
the cabinet is a toy lightsaber (red). Upstage-right is a door,
painted white. Upstage-centre, a black chair. Downstage-right,
a microphone.

At clearance – blackout. Then music evocative of nature
documentaries.

Slowly fade up to a spot on JOE, *at the microphone, in a dark-red*
dressing gown, pyjama bottoms and a Superman T-shirt. JOE *has*
the hood of his dressing gown up, and his hands in his sleeves, at
his waist, like a monk. Or a Jedi. He speaks into the microphone,
in a David Attenborough impression.

ATTENBOROUGH. Behold… the Fanboy. Raised on a diet of
popular culture, high-fructose snacks, and entitlement, the
Fanboy thrives in dark corners of the internet. Which can
make searching for a mate rather difficult.

Once considered a rare species, the Fanboy's numbers have
grown exponentially in the last decade, due to internet
forums, online gaming, and Disney buying both Marvel
Studios and *Star Wars*, in order to repackage and resell them
their childhood.

But it's not all good news for Fanboys. While their numbers
are strong, they remain vulnerable to threats from both
without, and within, their complex communities…

This particular Fanboy might appear to be joyful –
embracing nostalgia, harmlessly. But he is in fact using it to
hide from a deeply unhappy present –

ACT ONE

1.1

The nature documentary music cuts out, the lights snap to something much warmer and more present, as JOE *steps away from the microphone, takes his hood down, and smiles at the audience.*

JOE. Hello. I'm Joe. And I... am a bit of a nerd!

> JOE *pulls out a fold-down toy lightsaber (blue), concealed in the sleeve of his dressing gown, swinging it upwards so the parts of the saber click into place in one movement.*

> In my childhood, I was unaware of it. In my teens, I hid it. In my twenties, I owned it. I've just entered my thirties, and I'm coming to terms with the fact that I'm now older than most of the fictional characters in my favourite films, books and games.

> I have not, however, come to terms with the fact that I'm also older than the creators of my favourite films, books and games were, when they had their first major successes...

> JOE *retracts the lightsaber, and puts it down.*

> Things or people I am now or was once a fan of include, but are not limited to, the following:

> *Harry Potter*

> *Lord of the Rings*

> *Game of Thrones*

> *His Dark Materials*

> *Super Mario Bros.*

> *The Legend of Zelda*

> *Donkey Kong Country*

> The Labour Party

> The Green Party

> Mario Party

The New Statesman

The *Guardian*

Star Wars

In the following order of ascending quality:

Episodes XI, II, I, III, VII, VI, VIII, IV and *V.* Fight me.

He gathers momentum, talking rapidly.

Free Willy

The Foo Fighters

Prince

The RSBP

David Attenborough

Power Rangers

The Really Wild Show

Art Attack

Wallace and Gromit

Roald Dahl

Studio Ghibli

Everything Marvel has ever created…

He takes a deep breath.

…and *The West Wing.*

I like films, books and games where the goodies win against the baddies…

Blackout. JOE *approaches the microphone, and breathes into it like Darth Vader. We hear the 'zzzssshum' sound of a lightsaber firing up, as* JOE *is suddenly lit red and blue.*

Star Wars *fan-film:*

JOE *performs a mini-film of the* Star Wars Trilogy – *recreating iconic moments with lightning-fast, razor-sharp impressions. We whip through the galaxy in ninety seconds.*

The 'zzzssshum' of a lightsaber powering down. Lights return to normality.

1.2.

JOE. So, welcome to the show!

I am a bit of a magpie – I love collecting things. And I find it very hard to let go of things. So I brought some stuff with me, real things, from my old room – I wanted to sort of recreate it, like it was when I was a kid. I'll just talk you through a few of them now. First of all… a door!

I had a door when I was a kid – pretty cool!

This cabinet which is almost as old and almost as tall as I am. The TV, which is older than I am. But not as tall. I actually inherited this from my Uncle Obi, so I really fucking love this thing.

JOE *picks up a* Lord of the Rings *novel, a* Warhammer *rulebook, and a* Lord of the Rings Strategy Battle Game *rulebook.*

Books: *Lord of the Rings. Warhammer… Lord of the Rings Warhammer.* I also brought my old Sticky Tongue Jar Jar Binks toy, but I've lost that somewhere.

(*Shouting to the tech box.*) Dylan – did that turn up anywhere?

DYLAN (*shouting back from the tech box*). No, sorry!

JOE. Well, it's here somewhere… That's Dylan by the way – absolute legend!

The Super Nintendo! Which I keep in a box, because it's made from a certain kind of plastic, which discolours when it's exposed to direct sunlight. If you know, you know…

My old VHS player – fucking love this too!

Videotapes, including what I like to call the Christmas Trilogy, which if you don't know is *Die Hard*, *The Muppet Christmas Carol*, and *Home Alone*.

Anyone here a *Home Alone* fan? I fucking love it! Especially the part where Kevin uses a videotape of the gangster movie he's not allowed to watch but now can, because he's home alone, in order to trick the pizza delivery guy into believing he is not, in fact, home alone – pausing and rewinding and fast-forwarding in all the right places, to create the illusion of dialogue.

1.3

JOE. I brought another tape with me, which is simply labelled…

JOE *ejects a tape from the video player.*

Joe's Birthday Parties.

JOE *holds the tape aloft – we hear the* Legend of Zelda *treasure chest noise.*

This was made by my Uncle Obi, who had a video camera, which is something my parents couldn't afford. Obi would film family events, and he and I loved messing around – he'd get me to do interviews to the camera, that sort of thing. I think he was planning to edit my birthday parties, over the years, as I grew up, into a sort of memento, to give to me when I got older.

He never quite got around to finishing that.

But this tape starts with my eighth birthday party, which was a particularly epic one. Fancy dress: me dressed as Superman, my little brother dressed as Batman, my little sister dressed as Po – the Teletubby, not the *Star Wars* Resistance pilot, obviously…

JOE *puts the tape into the VHS player, picks up a remote control, and presses play.*

I'll play it for you now. *This* is me and the voice you can hear is my Uncle Obi:

The home recording plays on the TV. We hear OBI*'s voice, off-screen, and see* YOUNG JOE, *aged eight, in a Superman costume, running around his bedroom, then speaking to the camera.* JOE *watches the recording of his younger self.*

OBI. Hi Joe.

YOUNG JOE. Hi! Hello?

OBI. Do you want to, um, talk to the camera?

YOUNG JOE. Yeah… hello!

OBI. Are you having a nice birthday?

YOUNG JOE. Yes!

OBI. Have you had fun with your friends?

YOUNG JOE. Mmm… yes lots!

OBI. Did you get any nice presents?

YOUNG JOE. Yes!

OBI. What was your favourite part of today then, Joe?

YOUNG JOE. Dressing up as Superman!

OBI. And what are you having for dinner?

YOUNG JOE (*hesitates*). Pizza!

OBI (*laughing*). You don't sound very sure about that! What sort of pizza?

YOUNG JOE. Cheesy!

The video continues to play on the TV, with YOUNG JOE *still running around in his Superman costume.* JOE *moves downstage and grins at the audience.*

JOE. It's May 2nd 1997. It's six-thirty a.m., and I've officially been eight years old for four hours and seventeen minutes.

The news is on. Something important is happening:

Footage of Tony Blair, the 1997 election, cheering crowds, etc.

My parents try to explain what, but I'm not listening, because today I get the following presents:

The presents appear on the TV screen, as they're listed.

Donkey Kong Country, for the Super Nintendo,

Four books on wildlife:

– one about whales,

– one about killer whales,

– one about birds,

– and one about birds of prey

– (or as I call them: killer birds),

I also get a birdwatching kit, which includes:

– binoculars,

– notepads,

– a cassette tape called *Bird Songs of the British Isles*,

And a year's membership to the YOC!

I'm now a fledgling, card-carrying member of the Young Ornithologists' Club, the youth wing of the Royal Society for the Protection of Birds. Youth wing…

Sound of a bird call.

Anyone know what that is?

(*Depending on the response.*) It's a magpie…

Around this time, production is about to start on the new *Star Wars* film – *Episode I: The Phantom Menace* – the next instalment of George Lucas's Skywalker saga. Or, technically, the previous instalment.

The first time he watches the original trilogy with me, Uncle Obi tries to explain the chronology of the stories compared with the chronology of when the films were made, and why. And I stare back at him with the same blank expression that Jake Lloyd gives Liam Neeson when he tries to explain what Midi-chlorians are.

On the TV: the corresponding clip from Star Wars, Episode I: The Phantom Menace.

The originals Obi watches with me are the 1990s special-edition re-releases on VHS, which come in a special-edition, gold-coloured, Darth Vader sleeve.

On the TV: we see the videos. Then YOUNG JOE, *grinning.*

I'm too young to appreciate the full cultural significance of these films, but old enough to understand I am being shown something sacred, from the past.

Also around this time, in 1997, a young actor named Ahmed Best has been cast as a new character for the new film: a character called Jar Jar Binks. And millions of *Star Wars* fans around the world are using a piece of nascent technology called the internet, to eagerly discuss and speculate on what they consider to be the cultural event of a generation. But in 1997, I'm unaware of it, for two reasons.

One: I am not, yet, a *Star Wars* fan, though I do collect the *Star Wars* Tazos you get in packets of crisps, because I am a fan of crisps.

And two: I don't yet know what the internet is. Our council flat didn't have a landline until I was in primary school. We didn't get a computer until I was in secondary school, and we didn't get a modem and dial-up until even later.

Sound effect of a modem.

The initial reaction to *The Phantom Menace* from critics was mixed, but from fans it was, at least in box-office terms, record-breaking. Within months though, euphoria led to resentment and, as Master Yoda said…

On the TV: the corresponding clip of Yoda, from Revenge of the Sith, *speaking in time with* JOE.

…fear led to anger, anger led to hate, and hate led to suffering…

The TV flashes – YOUNG JOE *reappears, watching, grinning.*

But again, I was oblivious.

1.4

JOE *looks at us, conspiratorially. He has the VHS player remote in his hand.*

JOE. Hey Joe: do you want to say hello to the audience?

JOE *rewinds the video to the right place so that* YOUNG JOE *'answers'.*

YOUNG JOE. Yes!

JOE *pauses the video.*

JOE. Go on then.

JOE *rewinds the tape to:*

YOUNG JOE. Hello!

JOE *pauses the tape.*

JOE. Are you enjoying the show?

JOE *fast-forwards the tape to:*

YOUNG JOE. Mmm… yes lots.

JOE *pauses the tape.*

JOE. Anything it needs more of?

JOE *rewinds the tape to:*

YOUNG JOE. Dressing up as Superman!

JOE *pauses the tape.*

JOE. What do you think of me pausing and rewinding and fast-forwarding you in all the right places to create the illusion of dialogue?

JOE *fast-forwards the tape to:*

YOUNG JOE. Cheesy!

JOE *pauses the video, turns away from the TV, moves further downstage and smiles at the audience again.*

JOE. I didn't always consider myself a nerd –

YOUNG JOE. What's it like when I'm thirty?

JOE *glances back at the TV. His younger self is listening, innocently.* JOE *turns back to the audience and continues:*

JOE. I didn't always consider –

On the TV: the footage of YOUNG JOE *rewinds itself and plays:*

YOUNG JOE. Hello?

JOE *whips round again –* YOUNG JOE *is still. Innocent.* JOE *turns slowly back to the audience, then quickly looks back at the TV.* YOUNG JOE *still hasn't moved.* JOE *turns to the audience once more.*

JOE (*to audience*). I didn't –

On the TV: the footage of YOUNG JOE *rewinds itself and plays:*

YOUNG JOE. HELLO?!

JOE *looks round in time to see* YOUNG JOE *talking.*

JOE. Hello?

YOUNG JOE. Can you hear me?

JOE *looks at the TV, in shocked disbelief.*

JOE. Can *you* hear *me*?

YOUNG JOE. Yes.

JOE. Really?

YOUNG JOE. Yes!

The two JOES *stare at each other.* JOE *glances at the audience once more.*

So: what's it like when I'm thirty?

Beat.

JOE. How do you know I'm thirty?

YOUNG JOE. You look really grown up.

JOE. Is that a compliment?

YOUNG JOE. What's a compliment?

JOE. It means… a nice thing to say about someone.

YOUNG JOE. Then yes. So, what's it like?!

JOE. Fine… Everything's fine.

YOUNG JOE. Tell me about the games.

JOE *is suddenly excited, forgetting how odd this is. He moves the chair closer to the cabinet, and sits facing the TV.*

JOE. Oh my god, there's so much to tell you!

YOUNG JOE. What?!

JOE. So, you know Uncle Obi's Game Boy?

YOUNG JOE. Yeah.

JOE. And you know his Nintendo 64?

YOUNG JOE. Yeah

JOE. Well, imagine graphics that are ten times better than the N64, but you can take it around with you all the time, like a Game Boy, and plug it into your TV when you get home. That's how good games are now!

YOUNG JOE. Wow…

JOE. Yeah…

YOUNG JOE. Have you been to SeaWorld yet?

JOE. No – we don't want to go to SeaWorld any more.

YOUNG JOE. Why not?

JOE. Well… you know how in *Free Willy*, one of the messages of the film is that putting killer whales in captivity is bad?

YOUNG JOE. Yeah.

JOE. Well, it turns out that putting whales in captivity is bad.

YOUNG JOE. Oh. I should have made that connection! You know, orcas aren't whales – they're dolphins.

JOE. Yeah, I know.

YOUNG JOE. Do you still like Superman?

JOE. Sure. I prefer Spider-Man though.

YOUNG JOE. Why?

JOE. I just think he's more interesting.

YOUNG JOE. But Superman can do more stuff. Laser eyes, ice breath, super-strength, and he can fly! He's more powerful.

JOE. I guess that's my point. He's too good.

YOUNG JOE. How can you be too good?

JOE *is about to answer when the TV suddenly switches off.* JOE *tries to switch it back on. Nothing…*

1.5

JOE *turns to the audience once more, with a slightly baffled grin.*

JOE. That was… weird. This is meant to be a true story. Well, *based* on a true story. You know, like *The Social Network*. Or *Fargo*. Or *The Muppet Christmas Carol*. I changed the names. Except mine. Obviously.

JOE *thinks for a beat, then tentatively continues.*

And I should also probably disclose – this is my first time around this many people, in quite a while. I've just had some stuff… going on, in my personal life. I mean, I'm fine!

I've had a lot of time to myself – hundreds of hours of games to play: *Breath of the Wild*, *Fire Emblem*, *Odyssey* (*Mario Odyssey*, not *Assassin's Creed*, obviously). I've had all the Marvel, *Star Wars* and Muppets films in one place; everything David Attenborough has ever narrated… So I really am fine. Honestly.

Beat.

JOE *looks frustrated. He looks around.*

I still can't find my Jar Jar Binks Sticky Tongue Toy. I really wanted to show you that…

Uncle Obi got it for me.

Dad loved *Star Wars*. But Uncle Obi *fucking* loved it. And he somehow convinced Dad to let him take me to the midnight launch of *The Phantom Menace*, in 1999.

Lights change. JOE *flits between playing* DAD *and* OBI.

DAD. You want to take Joe to a film that starts three hours after his bedtime?

OBI. Yeah.

DAD. On a school night?

OBI. Yeah.

DAD. You know he's ten?

OBI. Mate, it's the cinematic event of a generation! You only ever get to watch something for the first time, once…

Beat.

DAD. Fine, but no sweets.

JOE. A man of his word, Obi buys us popcorn.

Lights change – we're in the cinema. JOE *moves the chair centre-stage and sits.*

The air-conditioning in the cinema is on overdrive for some reason, and I start to shiver, but I'm too excited to notice. Obi does notice, and lends me his jumper. It's a deep, rich purple, and so big on me that it's kind of like wearing a duvet.

We hear the 20th Century Fox drums and horns, and on the TV screen we see the corresponding 20th Century Fox logo. Then the blue words, then the yellow words from Star Wars.

As everything goes dark, and the hush descends, just before the yellow words start scrolling and John Williams' score kicks in – in that magical in-between – Obi and I look at each other, with big, stupid grins.

And it starts…

A moment, as JOE *takes in the film with childlike wonder.*

On the way out, Obi asks me what I thought.

JOE *leaps to his feet, suddenly with us once more.*

'I loved the lightsabers, I loved the podracing, I loved all the underwater stuff!' Obi grins and says he loved all of that too. Neither of us mention the taxation of galactic trade routes.

'And Jar Jar… I loved the funny things he said. His somersaults. How he accidentally blew up the droid tanks with those blue bouncing bombs. The way he caught bugs with his tongue!'

I've brought him with me – the toy – and I demonstrate, flicking the tongue forward. Now, the tongue on this toy was so sticky, you could use it to grab bits of paper or crisp packets. And as I flick it forward now, it latches onto a box of half-eaten popcorn, carried by a full-grown man walking beside us in full-length Jedi robes. The tongue wrenches the box right out of his hands and scatters the remaining popcorn across the carpet of the lobby. The man's response is to glare at me, from under his hood, with those eyes…

Obi apologises, quickly, expertly brushing over the moment, before it can escalate into anything else, ushering me out into the car park, asking me what else I loved about the film.

But the man's eyes, from under the hood, stay with me.

And I think about him sometimes. And I wonder: what was he really angry about?

Was it the popcorn – was he planning to take the rest of it home for his breakfast? Was it the film? Or was it something else?

Because it never occurred to me, leaving that cinema, that anyone else having watched the film we'd just watched, could have felt anything other than joy, and hope and love for the world.

ACT TWO

2.1

JOE. I didn't always consider myself a nerd. Or a Fanboy. I was just a boy. Sitting in front of a Super Nintendo. Asking Donkey Kong not to die so easily.

On the TV: Donkey Kong Country *'GAME OVER' screen, and the 'death' sound.*

I was just a fan of things. I liked what I liked. I wasn't embarrassed by my own interests and hobbies. I liked stuff whole-heartedly. I didn't critique it. I just fucking loved it.

But like everyone, as I move into adolescence, I discover nuance and variation. And that other wonderful thing that all teenage boys discover. The thing that keeps them locked in their rooms, alone, for hours on end. W... *Warhammer*.

I become an awkward teenager. I start to feel like I'm at the window, looking in at life, nose against the glass, too nervous to knock.

I'm the guy reading *Lord of the Rings* in the corner of the playground, instead of playing football, sneaking *Star Wars* Tazos in like contraband, with no one to swap them with. Scribbling Tyranids Vs Blood Angels army lists inside my maths book, for a battle that would never take place.

I love toys, books, films and games to the point of obsession: physical things, fictional worlds. But I struggle with people.

Beat – a moment of vulnerability.

I guess some things never change...

JOE *catches himself, brightens up again, trying to brush over what just happened.*

Sorry, that was completely unnecessary – I really am fine! And sharing these memories with you is lovely: nothing cheers me up like reminiscing, especially about *Star Wars*. So, let's crack on with the show!

2.2

JOE. It's 2006. And I am at a party. Somehow.

Party noises/music in the background.

I've just started my A levels, miles away from home, because my school doesn't have a sixth form. I'm trying to blend into the corner, clutching a can of Carling like a Chewbacca teddy. A couple of people I vaguely recognise are chatting video games.

I cautiously join their conversation. One person in the group – Wayne – mentions the comedy series *Peep Show*, and then the sketch comedy show, starring the same leading actors: *That Mitchell and Webb Look*.

(*Shouting over the noise*.) I fucking love that show!

Wayne's eyes light up:

WAYNE. Oh my god same! I LOVE the Nazis!

JOE. What? Oh, the sketch!

(*Aside, to audience*.) He's talking about a sketch – David Mitchell and Robert Webb play these German soldiers in World War Two. Wayne and I start quoting it at one another:

JOE *and* WAYNE *act out the 'Are We the Baddies?' sketch from* That Mitchell and Webb Look.

Everyone else kind of moves on, but Wayne and I get talking about *Star Wars*. We just *know* – like we're Force-sensitive!

Someone batch-cooks toast on the grill, forgets about it and sets the smoke alarm off.

JOE *stands on the chair.*

I stand on a chair to turn it off, which is unremarkable in itself, but the deafening noise, followed by the sudden silence, and the fact I'm now the tallest person in the room, means I have an audience, after years of making myself invisible. Something strange comes over me: I feel like Luke, switching off his targeting computer. I grab a rolling pin from the sideboard, point it at Wayne and say:

JOE (KENOBI). It's finished, Wayne – I've got the high ground!

JOE. The room stays silent. Wayne stares, impassive. He could leave me to die on this chair, we both know it. But he grins, grabs an empty kitchen-roll tube, points it at me and says:

WAYNE (ANAKIN). Joe – you've underestimated my abilities!

Music rises – 'Anakin vs. Obi Wan' by John Williams.

JOE. And we re-enact the entire scene above the fires of Mustafar!

They act out the scene – two man-children swinging lightsabers at one another in a deadly duel, making their own sound effects – grunts, shouts and 'zzzssshums'.

JOE *steps down from the chair.*

(*To us.*) This music, though, am I right?! This fucking music! And when it's time for me to cut off his limbs, and leave him to slide into the lava, Wayne really goes for it: he grabs the burned toast, crunches it up, smears charcoal all over his face and writhes on the floor in pain and anguish –

WAYNE. AAAAAAAAAGHH!

JOE. People are applauding and cheering. I help him up, and he slaps my back in a kind of manly hug and says –

WAYNE. Mate, it's so good to finally meet someone who hates the prequels as much as I do!

Music cuts out suddenly. JOE *looks stunned.*

JOE. I blink.

WAYNE. It's a particular kind of obsession, isn't it? To hate something so much you watch it, over and over – so much you *almost* love it?

JOE. And I feel so accepted and included, that even though *that* is the opposite of what I think, I tell Wayne:

'That's exactly what I think! I fucking hate the prequels.'

From that moment on, Wayne and I are inseparable. Through the rest of sixth form. We live together, during my gap year, before I go away. We make all these grand plans for the future. And the prequels: I lose count of how many times we rewatch them. Wayne teaches me everything that's wrong with them.

'Wow. Yeah. They're worse than I remember…'

At this point, I still have my *Phantom Menace* poster on my bedroom wall and my Jar Jar Sticky Tongue Toy on my desk – 'ironically', of course. Wayne, I'm pretty sure, believes that line, and seems to find it funny. And if I can make Wayne laugh, I feel amazing about myself. He has these eyes full of quiet rage, a face in a state of perpetual irritation. But if I can make him laugh, especially about *Star Wars*, I see something change in his eyes. I catch a glimpse – just a glimpse – of the little boy I imagined he used to be.

And during this phase of my life, when I'd rewatch the prequels endlessly with Wayne, and trash-talk them, I'd do something else to make him laugh – I would describe ways in which Jar Jar Binks – the character – would die. I'd say things like:

'Fuck off, Jar Jar. Do us all a favour and eat that blue, bouncing bomb so we can watch your stupid Gungan brains splatter over Naboo.'

Sure, it was a bit mean, but it was just banter – it was just us.

'Jar Jar, you serve no purpose!'

'Jar Jar, you're useless! Jar Jar, you're pointless! Jar Jar, you ruined my childhood!'

'Jar Jar, you're a fucking waste of space!'

Beat.

Stuff like that. And Wayne would laugh. And I'd feel like we were in a club.

But a quiet, creeping feeling would prod at me, like R2-D2 with something annoying but important to say. A question, really:

'Were we the baddies?'

I think, when I first saw Jar Jar –

VOICE. Hello? Can you hear me?

JOE. Dylan… I don't think there's a sound cue there.

DYLAN. Yeah sorry, I don't know what happened there.

VOICE. This stupid old piece of junk…

JOE. Dylan?

DYLAN. I think it was some sort of interference. It's gone now.

JOE. Okay – thanks…

2.4

JOE. I think when I first saw Jar Jar Binks, I must have been the right age. Or maybe I saw him as an eco-warrior – trying to save his planet from the perils of technology. Or perhaps it was the other way around.

I wonder the same thing about David Attenborough: is he a hero, to me, because I love the natural world? Or do I love the natural world because David Attenborough's a hero?

Or maybe I loved Jar Jar because I love animals. Which is the main reason I fucking love *Donkey Kong Country* – every character in that game is an animal. Even the baddies – the Kremlins – are crocodiles.

YOUNG JOE *appears on the TV. He looks older, his hair longer, wearing something different.*

YOUNG JOE. Crocodilians.

JOE. What?

YOUNG JOE. Crocodilians, not crocodiles.

JOE. Crocodilians isn't a word.

YOUNG JOE. It's the name for the family that crocodiles belong to.

JOE. Okay…

YOUNG JOE. They include caimans, alligators and crocodiles, obviously.

JOE. It's a game. I'm talking about a game. It's pretend.

YOUNG JOE. You should still get it right.

JOE. Look sometimes the detail doesn't matter. It's the feeling, the memory that's important. Can you please just let me have that?

Beat.

YOUNG JOE. I don't really know what you're talking about.

JOE *notices* YOUNG JOE *is holding a Jar Jar Sticky Tongue Toy.*

JOE. Hang on… is that my Jar Jar Sticky Tongue Toy?

YOUNG JOE. It's *my* Jar Jar Sticky Tongue Toy!

JOE. I've been searching everywhere for that!

(*To us.*) It's always in the last place you look, isn't it – inside a magic videotape from the past…

YOUNG JOE. What?

JOE. Nothing. I was trying to make a joke.

YOUNG JOE. It wasn't very funny.

JOE. It was very funny. Seriously, how have you got that?!

YOUNG JOE (*shrugs*). The Force?!

JOE *stares.*

JOE (*remembering*). That was a promotional toy, just before *Episode I* came out. And you look like you're… ten, in this video? Have you seen it yet?

YOUNG JOE. No but I'm seeing it tomorrow! It's going to be the best *Star Wars* film ever. Probably the best film in the whole world of all time. I'm so excited… YAAAAAAY!

JOE *smiles to himself.*

JOE. Well… I hope you enjoy it.

YOUNG JOE (*gasps*). Have *you* seen it?!

JOE. What do you think?

YOUNG JOE. Oh yeah, you must have – cos you're old! So?!

JOE. So what?!

YOUNG JOE. Tell me what happens!

JOE. No.

YOUNG JOE. Why not?!

JOE. You're seeing it tomorrow!

YOUNG JOE. Yeah. But I want to know!

JOE. Won't that spoil the surprise?

YOUNG JOE. No. Tell me! I can't wait.

JOE. You can't wait a day?

YOUNG JOE. A day's a long time when you're a kid.

> YOUNG JOE *runs off. The TV turns itself off.* JOE *stares. He turns to the audience once more.*

ACT THREE

3.1

JOE. When the *Star Wars* sequel trilogy was announced, Wayne and I made a pact that no matter where we were living, or what we were doing, we would go and see the midnight launch of all three of those new films, together.

We're at the cinema – the buzz of anticipation.

So, it's December, 2015, I'm at the midnight launch of *Star Wars Episode VII: The Force Awakens…* and I'm on my own. I moved away, years ago. Wayne still lives at home. We just don't keep in touch as much as we used to.

But of course, I'm not alone. Because even if I don't know anyone here, everyone who is here, is here for the same reason.

And there's something magical about that. Something that reminds me of the midnight launch, with Obi, all those years ago.

It's things like… those two dickheads with the lightsabers. Or that couple with the kid in the Wookie mask, who's clearly up way past his bedtime, but that is the kind of parenting I aspire to!

Or the person sat next to me, in her Jar Jar Binks T-shirt.

JOE *sits. He glances at the person next to him.*

It's a cool T-shirt.

He looks again.

It's a really cool T-shirt…

As everything goes dark and the hush descends, just before John Williams' score kicks in and the yellow words start scrolling – in that magical in-between – there is the tiniest look between us: something like 'this is it' crossed with 'it better be good.'

And it starts…

JOE *gazes out beyond the audience, as if at a vast cinema screen, with childlike wonder.*

During the film itself, I don't dare tear my eyes away from the screen for a second. But I never forget she's sat next to me.

JOE *stands. We're in the cinema lobby – a different kind of buzz.*

Afterwards, she's loitering in the lobby, looking at her phone.

He looks once more.

It's a *really* cool T-shirt…

JOE *nervously approaches.*

What happened to Jar Jar?

GAIA. Sorry?

JOE. Jar Jar Binks – wasn't in the film.

GAIA *realises he's talking about her T-shirt.*

GAIA. Oh! Yeah. I know. Gutted.

JOE, *lost in this memory, searches for the right words.*

The TV turns itself on, and YOUNG JOE *interrupts.*

YOUNG JOE. How tall am I when I grow up?

JOE *tries to stay in the cinema, but we're being pulled away from it.*

JOE. Quite tall.

YOUNG JOE. How tall?

JOE. Five feet eleven inches and three-quarters.

YOUNG JOE. So that's just a quarter off six feet?

JOE. Yes.

YOUNG JOE. That's annoying.

JOE. It's *really* annoying.

YOUNG JOE. Can't you just tell people you're six feet?

JOE. No, I tried.

YOUNG JOE. Surely they don't know?

JOE. Yeah, but I do and they can see it in my eyes.

YOUNG JOE. Do you have a six pack?

JOE. Absolutely not.

YOUNG JOE. Are you rich?

JOE. In the ways that matter.

YOUNG JOE. Yeah, but are you?

JOE. No.

> JOE *turns his attention away from the TV.*

YOUNG JOE. What you doing?

JOE. I'm just… enjoying a memory.

YOUNG JOE. Ah, thanks!

JOE. No, not with you. With someone else.

YOUNG JOE. Who?

JOE. Doesn't matter.

YOUNG JOE. Tell me.

JOE. No.

YOUNG JOE. Tell me.

JOE. No.

YOUNG JOE. Please?!

JOE. No!

YOUNG JOE. Why not?

> JOE *turns to face the TV.*

JOE. I don't like spoilers.

YOUNG JOE. What does that mean?

JOE. It means you'll enjoy it more if you just find out for yourself.

> YOUNG JOE *is about to respond, but* JOE *takes the remote and turns off the TV.*

3.2

Suddenly, we're back in the cinema lobby.

GAIA. Do you know the fan theory about him?

JOE (*still distracted from* YOUNG JOE'*s interruption*). Uhhh... who?

GAIA. Jar Jar Binks: the character you literally just asked me about...

JOE. Right! Sorry! Uhm... which one?

GAIA. That he's secretly a Sith Lord!

JOE. Oh yeah, so weird...

GAIA. I know! I hope they make a Jar Jar spin-off series: I fucking love the prequels.

    JOE *comes out of the memory, turns to us.*

JOE. 'I fucking love the prequels'?

GAIA. They're not perfect. But I love how they make me feel.

JOE (*aside, to us*). It's like I have permission to feel something I'd forgotten I even felt. Permission to think for myself.

    We're back in the memory.

GAIA. I love how Palpatine moves, in the shadows, manipulating everyone. Not just with Sith powers but with rhetoric, populism, creating conflict; presenting himself as the solution. It's flawed, but I really respect it for trying to say something about democracy and power and corruption in a film about, you know, space wizards!

JOE (*aside, to us*). I sort of stare, like a puppy. She saves me from myself:

GAIA. And then of course, Padmé has the best line of the trilogy.

JOE. Yeah – in the Senate, in *Revenge of the Sith*!

GAIA. Right?!

JOE (*aside, to us*). It's when Palpatine declares the Republic is now his Empire, and everyone's applauding except Padmé. She tells me about a deleted scene where Padmé tries to overthrow Palpatine before he can take full control of the galaxy, conspiring with Princess Leia's future adoptive father, Bail Organa.

JOE. Yeah! Played by… Jimmy Smits!

GAIA. Senator Santos, in *The West Wing*!

JOE. President Santos, please!

GAIA. Spoiler alert!

JOE (*to us*). We go from *Star Wars*, to *The West Wing*, to heroes, to politics, and everything in-between. We move on to the dark side of fandom:

GAIA. I think it's because most of them were bullied as kids. But they always had *Star Wars*…

JOE.…and now they think they own the space…

GAIA.…so they can bully other people out of that space…

JOE.…and cos they were bullied once, they couldn't possibly be the bullies…

GAIA.…exactly! It's like they have impunity. It's why I love Kylo Ren's character: obsessed with the past, desperate for control, smashing up his keyboard with his lightsaber when he doesn't get his way – he's like a proper 'fuck you' to all that!

We're out of the memory for a moment, as JOE *turns to us once more.*

JOE. It's like my eyes are open again, letting in the light, looking at the world; feeling excited and hopeful that it was meant for us, and that we could change it.

It feels like someone asking me to join the Rebellion.

Back in the memory once more: JOE *turns toward* GAIA, *more confidently.*

I'm Joe, by the way.

GAIA. Nice to meet you.

JOE. What's your name?

GAIA. Gaia.

They smile for a moment.

3.3

YOUNG JOE *appears on the screen, breaking the memory.*

YOUNG JOE. Who's that?

JOE. She's… just someone who…

YOUNG JOE. Is she your girlfriend?!

JOE. This is a really big spoiler.

YOUNG JOE. I want to know!

JOE. You're a kid – don't you find this weird?

YOUNG JOE. No.

JOE. Alright. What's your girlfriend's name?

YOUNG JOE. Eugh, yuck! I don't have a girlfriend!

JOE. See, you do find it weird.

YOUNG JOE. Yeah but *you* should have a girlfriend.

JOE. Why?

YOUNG JOE. Cos you're old.

JOE. Thanks.

YOUNG JOE. Maybe you should even be married.

JOE. Well, we're not married, so…

YOUNG JOE. Are you moving in together?

JOE. What?

YOUNG JOE. Apparently that's called living in sin…

JOE. Who says that?!

YOUNG JOE.…but I don't really know what that means…

Beat. JOE *is lost for words.*

JOE. Well, it means –

YOUNG JOE. Is that why you're sorting through your old stuff? Because you're moving in together, so you have to get rid of all your nerdy boy things?

JOE. Where on earth did you hear that?

YOUNG JOE (*shrugs*). I watch a lot of *Friends*.

JOE. Course you do…

YOUNG JOE. Do you want to play *Donkey Kong Country*?

JOE. I would love to play *Donkey Kong Country* with you – that would really cheer me up.

> *Beat.*

> But I'm in the middle of something right now, so…

YOUNG JOE. Alright, well I'm going to play it.

> YOUNG JOE *runs off the screen, leaving the empty background of the garden fence.*

JOE (*sarcastic, slightly offended*). Alright. See you later then.

> *Sudden blackout.*

> *A bluish, hooded* FIGURE *is projected onto the door. So briefly we barely see it.*

FIGURE. Joe… you must face the truth… you have to change the past…

> JOE *turns, just as the projection vanishes.* JOE *turns back to us, haunted.*

JOE. Dylan – what was that?

DYLAN (*from the tech box*). Sorry: don't know what happened there.

JOE (*to audience*). Sorry!

> *Beat.*

3.4

JOE. Gaia. Wayne. Obi.

I didn't just love them. I worshipped them. I was, to be honest, obsessed with them.

The past is a pretty magical place. But here, now: I'm like… a ghost… of myself.

Beat. JOE *sits.*

Wayne and Gaia met once. I was terrified: I just wanted them to like each other as much as I loved both of them. The first few pints are pretty good. I steer the conversation away from the prequels, obviously. And then Wayne starts to explain something called Gamergate.

WAYNE (*gently, at first like* JOE *and* GAIA *will agree with him*). What it is, right what it is yeah, what it is, right. What it is… people, 'arts journalists' – wading into something they don't understand, and saying that cos Mario rescues a princess, or you can sleep with a hooker in GTA5, we're all gonna turn into sexist pigs or something: cos clearly we can't think for ourselves!

GAIA. Sure… but I think it is important to question tropes. And stereotypes. What that says about society, how it might influence players – young players especially – players of all genders.

WAYNE. Both.

GAIA. Sorry?

WAYNE. You mean both genders.

GAIA. No. I mean all.

A tense beat.

JOE. I try and steer the conversation on to something else, but they've dug in. It's like rebels in the trenches of Hoth on one side, and Stormtroopers and AT-ATs on the other.

WAYNE. It's just… there's corruption in the games industry, okay?! People are trying to call it out.

GAIA. Right… but sharing someone's address online? Making death threats? You think that's okay, do you?

WAYNE (*angrier*). Obviously not. But it doesn't mean I have to agree with a radical feminist agenda, does it?!

JOE. I say very little. They never meet again. When I'm with one of them, we avoid talking about the other.

ACT FOUR

4.1

JOE *closes his eyes, leans back in the chair.*

JOE. It's spring 2016. I'm dreaming. I'm at Helm's Deep.
Thousands of Uruk-hai marching towards me. Gimli,
Legolas, Aragorn are nowhere to be seen. An orc climbs the
battlements, sword raised, mouth snarling, about to –

Phone rings. JOE *wakes with a start.*

It's Dad. Dad never calls in the morning.

DAD. Joe… I've got some really bad news. It's Uncle Obi.

JOE. Through a mix of shock and sleep inertia, I ask him to say
it twice.

DAD. He died.

Silence.

I'm really sorry, mate.

JOE. 'Dad. I don't… I don't know what to say.'

We share memories for a little while. Dad reminds me of a
Christmas Eve when I was about fourteen, when he and Obi
let me, my brother and our cousins try Jack Daniel's and
Coke for the first time.

DAD. Just one, mind.

JOE. And within about three hours the six of us are in a happy,
wobbly huddle, singing our hearts out to 'Purple Rain'. Dad
and Obi fucking loved Prince.

'Purple Rain' by Prince starts playing.

I remind Dad about the midnight launch of *The Phantom
Menace* Obi took me to, all those years ago. I tell him about
the popcorn. Dad gives a sort of choked laugh. When we get
off the phone, I send him a picture of the purple jumper Obi
lent me that night, which I never gave back.

Later on, Gaia listens to 'Purple Rain' with me, not saying anything.

The music fades out.

I start to wonder how we can carry on without our heroes. Who's going to lead us, who's going to save us?

How have we lost Prince, Bowie and Alan Rickman in the same horrible spring, but Farage and Trump are still loud and thriving?!

And now Obi…

There was a meme that did the rounds that year, as our heroes died and the world spun off its axis, a meme that said:

MEME. Someone find David Attenborough and keep him safe.

JOE. Everything feels so weird. So wrong. (*Softly – confused.*) And why is Wayne clogging up my social media feed with all these videos of angry men? Who's Ben Shapiro? Who's Joe Rogan? Who's Jordan Peterson? Who are these people? Where did he find this… club? How big is it? How deep does it go? And what *exactly* are they so angry about?

But Wayne does call me, when he hears about Obi.

'Mate. Thanks for ringing. I just… I don't… I can't…'

WAYNE. I know.

JOE. And he does know. To be fair to him, he really does know. And those two words were all he needed to say.

The problem was, between that phone call and the next time I see Wayne, a lot of things happen:

JOE *moves to the microphone – the following plays out like the mini-film from earlier.*

NEWSREADER. The starting guns have been fired on the referendum for Britain's membership of the European Union.

FARAGE. I want my country back!

NEWSREADER. The MP, Jo Cox, was murdered today. Her attacker, who had links to several far-right groups, shot and stabbed the mother of two multiple times –

JOE. What the fuck is happening?

JOHNSON. Let's Take Back Control!

JOE. Gaia and I stay up to watch the result together. We've brought snacks, we've brought ice cream. At about two a.m. we take the ice cream out of the freezer to soften before we eat it. The results are looking…

GAIA. No. Surely not… it can't be…

JOE. At about three a.m. I remember the ice cream and suggest we eat our anxiety. But we left it too long, we got complacent, it's melted into a sickly, gloopy, mess.

DIMBLEBY. We're now calling it. The UK's decision taken in 1975 to join the common market has been reversed…

JOE. We try to salvage what we have, we put the ice cream back in the freezer, but it's too late – the damage has been done, what's done cannot be undone –

FARAGE. And we'll have done it, without a single bullet having been fired…

JOE. I feel sick.

I think surely this year cannot get any worse, then:

TRUMP. You know, when you're a star they let you do whatever you want…

JOE. The phrase 'locker-room talk' makes me think about things I said to Wayne when we'd trash-talk the prequels. It makes me glad there wasn't a microphone, or that anyone put it online.

TRUMP. It's time to dream big, for our country. God bless America.

JOE *moves away from the microphone.*

JOE. And like a lot of people, by November 2016, I feel frightened. About what all of this means for climate change. For human rights. For democracy.

And I think I could have just about coped, if Wayne wasn't so fucking elated. What is it exactly he thinks he's won, from all of this? And if he has won, why is he still so angry?

When I go back for Christmas that year, we watch *Rogue One* together, but afterwards, when Wayne suggests going for a pint, I decline. I don't trust myself to not talk about any of that – (*Gestures towards microphone.*) We still have *Star Wars*, and I want to keep it that way.

'So… I thought that was decent? You?'

WAYNE. Yeah. Decent. Sure you don't want a pint?

Beat.

JOE. I should get going.

WAYNE. Alright. See ya.

JOE. Wayne?

WAYNE. Yeah?

JOE. I thought it was pretty damn good actually. Considering it's all based on a throwaway line from *Return of the Jedi*.

WAYNE. Yeah – a whole film about many Bothans, who died getting the plans…

JOE. Poor Manny Bothans – he was such a lovely guy.

Wayne laughs. I catch a glimpse of the little boy, behind his eyes, again. I can still make him laugh. We still have *Star Wars*, and as long as we do, there's still hope…

4.2

JOE. Christmas 2016 is our first without Obi. And it's really, fucking weird. This whole year's been a blur, the whole world is on fire, and I just want to tune out, hide, pretend that the following year isn't coming to devour us all. I try and lose myself in my favourite Christmas film, and to be honest one of my favourite films of all time…

JOE *moves to the microphone.*

He re-enacts the following lines from Charles Dickens'
A Christmas Carol, *using Muppet and Michael Caine impressions:*

'He was a tight-fisted hand at the grindstone, Scrooge!
A squeezing, wrenching, grasping, scraping, clutching,
covetous old sinner.'

'If they would rather die, they had better do it, and decrease
the surplus population.'

'Why do you doubt your senses?'

'I am the Ghost of Christmas Past.'

JOE *covers the microphone with his hand, glares at the
audience.*

By the way, why did they cut the break-up song 'When Love
is Gone' out of the DVD version?! Rizzo the Rat is crying for
absolutely no reason now, and when they sing 'When Love is
Found' at the end of the film it's no longer a reprise, a
callback, to show how the protagonist has changed and unify
the themes of the story, it's just a song. And yes it's a nice
song but it just meant so much more to me when I was a kid!

JOE *continues talking into the mic:*

'Come in, and know me better, man!'

'The Founder of the Feast, indeed!'

'My dear, the children! Christmas Day!'

'What then? If he be like to die, he had better do it, and
decrease the surplus population.'

'What's to-day, my fine fellow?'

'To-day?! Why, it's Christmas Day!'

'And to Tiny Tim, WHO DID NOT DIE, he became as good
a friend, as good a master, as a good a man, as the good old
city knew.'

'God bless us, every one!'

JOE *moves away from the microphone.*

I will not hear a bad word said against *The Muppet Christmas
Carol*: the songs are perfect, the jokes are on-brand, it uses the
full weight and humour of the Muppets to bring that story to
life and there will never be a better version of that book than
this film.

Ever.

And so, on Christmas Day 2016, I insist that we do not watch *Home Alone 2: Lost in New York*, because Donald Trump is in it, and we instead watch *The Muppet Christmas Carol* an extra time (we already watched it on Christmas Eve, obviously).

But about halfway through I remember that Michael Caine campaigned for Brexit on the basis that:

MICHAEL CAINE (*into the microphone*). I'd rather be a poor master, than a rich servant.

JOE. And that's when I realised – everyone was either in my club now. Or they weren't. And if they weren't, I fucking hated them.

Beat.

4.3

JOE. 2016 ends with the news that Carrie Fisher has suffered a heart attack, but may yet pull through.

The last thing I read, doomscrolling, on Boxing Day is a parody headline – 'You're not taking Princess Leia as well, 2016 told.'

But I wake up the next morning to a real headline: that this horrible year has indeed claimed one more hero.

As I stumble through 2017, I see division everywhere. In everything. We can't accept each other's differences.

We can't peacefully coexist.

We can't even tolerate each other.

We only deal in absolutes.

I start to feel, like Anakin did, that if people weren't with me, they were the enemy.

On the TV: corresponding footage of Anakin from Revenge of the Sith.

We can't talk to each other. We can only shout.

It's like… a period of civil war.

So, when we finally make it to the end of the year, to December 2017, when Gaia and I go to the midnight launch of *The Last Jedi*, it feels like fleeing a TIE fighter ambush, and escaping into hyperspace.

Beat.

We spot a couple in old, faded *Star Wars* T-shirts, with their children, in shiny new *Star Wars* T-shirts. We smile. Gaia wonders if that might be us one day. Calm. Casual. Like it'd be the best thing ever but also the most normal thing in the world.

There's something so pure and magical about this many people, coming together to share the same moment – the same joy, the same hope, the same love.

It feels sacred.

And our post-film debrief is as giddy and glorious as our one two years prior.

GAIA. That line about failure!

JOE. Yoda as a puppet!

GAIA. The dice!

JOE. The Force-projection!

GAIA. The Porgs!

JOE. I read about those – they were puffins, on the Skelligs, where they filmed, and it was going to cost the same amount to CGI them out as it was to just CGI them into space-birds!

GAIA. Cute! Oh and the hyperspeed-kamikaze-crash where it all went silent!

JOE. And the lightsaber fight in the throne room!

GAIA. Thoughts on Canto Bight?

JOE. I… enjoyed it. Holdo?

GAIA. Legend!

JOE. And the kid grabbing the broom with the Force, at the end!

GAIA. Yes! *Anyone* can be Force-sensitive. We don't need dynasties!

JOE. Exactly! I fucking love it.

GAIA. I fucking love you!

JOE. But not everyone liked seeing their hero turn his back on the Force and abandon hope. Almost instantly, angry Fanboys are posting things online like: '#NotMyLuke' and 'this film is a complete cinematic failure' and '*The Last Jedi* ruined my childhood.'

I start to wonder why people are as divided over this film as they are about everything else.

I wonder how we could watch the same story, and feel such different things. Because to me *The Last Jedi* is the opposite of a complete cinematic failure – though it has some excellent things to say about failure – and I fucking love it.

4.4

Blackout. The projection of the hooded figure reappears on the door. We can only see his nose, mouth and grey-bearded chin – his eyes are covered by his hood. He's like a blue hologram of Obi Wan Kenobi. Or Emperor Palpatine.

FIGURE. No he doesn't. It's shit.

JOE *turns to see the figure on the door. He turns to* DYLAN, *panicked.*

JOE. Dylan, there's no projection in this show…

DYLAN (*from the tech box*). I literally don't know what's happening!

FIGURE. *The Last Jedi* is shit. And you know it's shit. You pretended to like it at the time so Gaia would like you, and you're pretending to like it now so the audience will like you.

JOE. Who are you?! What makes you think you know what's going on inside my head?

The figure laughs like Emperor Palpatine. JOE looks very shaken.

Beat. He glances back at the audience once more.

I hate that it's infected even this. That *Star Wars* has become a proxy in this endless culture war. That we can't even like a film about space wizards any more. We can't just sit together in a cinema and eat popcorn and watch X-wings blow up TIE fighters and goodies defeat baddies with laser swords. We have to see ourselves as heroes and everyone else as villains.

Wayne hates it. I knew he'd hate it – as soon as I saw that backlash online, I knew Wayne would be right there, all over it.

We always had this. No matter what else had happened we always had *Star Wars*. I scroll through his timeline. It's like he went to the midnight launch of *The Last Jedi* and then vowed not to sleep again until he'd told every single person on the internet exactly how wrong they were about everything. And it starts with this film, but it goes all the way back to the prequels, like they're some kind of childhood trauma he has to play out again and again and again.

And if I could change one thing, I'd have stopped scrolling.

Because once I saw it, I couldn't unsee it.

4.5

JOE *moves the chair and sits. We're in a pub. A dull hum of voices, clinking of glasses.*

JOE. Thanks for meeting.

WAYNE. Course. It's been a while.

JOE. Yeah. So… I saw your tweet.

WAYNE. What tweet?

JOE. 'Ahmed Best… eat that blue bouncing bomb so we can watch your stupid brains splatter all over New York.'

WAYNE (*laughs*). You annoyed I didn't credit you?

JOE. I thought that was a joke. Between us. About the character. You tweeted it to the real person.

WAYNE. So?

JOE. So are you going to take it down?

WAYNE. It's just banter.

JOE. 'Ahmed Best, you serve no purpose.'

'Ahmed Best, you're useless. Ahmed Best, you're pointless. Ahmed Best, you ruined my childhood.'

'Ahmed Best, you're a fucking waste of space.'

Beat.

You meant what you said. And you know what it did.

WAYNE. He didn't do that cos of me.

JOE. Are you even sorry?

WAYNE. No.

JOE (*to audience*). I become a little desperate now.

(*To* WAYNE.) Wayne... we've all said and done things we regret. Maybe at the time you weren't to know. So... if you do regret it, if you want to take it down, if you want to learn from it...

WAYNE (*laughing, disbelief*). Learn from it?! Listen to yourself! Do you think you're better than me? (*Bitter laugh, as he realises that is what* JOE *thinks*.) *You* said those things. You think you've got it all figured out – all the answers. Well, you don't. (*Rising anger.*) You've lost, mate. You're on the wrong side. Take the red pill: cos no one wants your liberal, snowflake, radical feminist agenda any more.

JOE. Wayne, this wasn't a fictional character. This was the real person who played that character and this person really tried to... he almost killed himself.

WAYNE. Didn't go through with it though, did he? He chickened out.

JOE. Are you –

WAYNE. I'm not sorry. I don't regret it. And I'm not going to take it down.

JOE (*to us*). He's resolute. Gripping his half-finished pint, white knuckles. Staring at me with that quiet rage in his eyes. I stare back. I look for the boy. I can't see him.

(*To* WAYNE.) Then... I'm really sorry, but I don't think we can be friends any more.

(*To us*.) For the briefest of moments, I think I do see him – the boy. Lost. Alone. Afraid. But I blink and he's gone. Wayne necks the rest of his pint, slams the glass down, and smirks.

WAYNE (*hint of a smug laugh*). Why are you sorry? We haven't been friends for years.

4.6

JOE *stands, back in the room with us once more.*

JOE. Gaia and I always talked about going to Iceland. To visit filming locations from *Game of Thrones*. To see puffins; to see where the ancient Viking parliament was held – at Thingvellir! And, if we're very, *very* lucky, killer whales. And in May 2019, we make it.

JOE *sits. We're in the memory.*

I'm a terrible navigator. So Gaia is map-reading, while I drive. She's filming me – we've just finished an orca-watching trip, and she wants to capture my disbelief that we really saw them. In the wild, with our own eyes...

Our playlist is on shuffle. 'Purple Rain' is finishing.

We hear the 'Purple Rain' guitar solo.

...Gaia looks out of her window:

GAIA. That's strange...

JOE. What?

GAIA. My map says there's a glacier, just there. But I can't see it.

JOE. Maybe we're too close to that hill?

GAIA. Yeah, maybe…

The end of the 'Purple Rain' guitar solo screeches out.

ACT FIVE

5.1

JOE. It's December 2019.

> JOE *moves to the microphone.*

JOHNSON. This morning, I went to Buckingham Palace. And I'm forming a new government. Thank you all, very much and Happy Christmas!

JOE. I'm exhausted from knocking doors. And I'm angry.

> Maybe I should have knocked more.
>
> Maybe I needn't have bothered.
>
> I'm at the midnight launch of *Rise of Skywalker*. Alone.
>
> I want to like it so much. I try to go in with an open mind, to relax and enjoy the ride. And I do enjoy the ride – it's a fun ride…
>
> …but… SPOILER ALERT!!!

> *The TV turns itself on. A 'SPOILER ALERT' warning flashes on the screen*

> (*Lightning speed.*) They seem to be going to every effort to reverse decisions made in *The Last Jedi*. People keep dying and coming back to life which means there's no real cost to anything. They bring Palpatine back from the dead like a video game final boss, overpowered, level nine hundred and ninety-nine –

PALPATINE (*into the microphone*). I can conjure a thousand Star Destroyers and crash all your friends' ships with lightning ahahaha!

JOE (*to us again, angrier, faster*). They don't just bring him back, they make him Rey's grandfather, and something I loved about *The Last Jedi* was how it moved away from bloodlines and dynasties and inherited power, and towards the idea that anyone could be Force-sensitive, and that heroes could really come from anywhere, which is surely in the spirit of the original *Star Wars* movie anyway – (*Shouting*.) and it all just makes me think:

For fuck's sake, *Rise of Skywalker*, you ruined my childhood!

I fucking hate it!

JOE *holds himself with anger, power. He grins manically at the audience.*

God, it feels good to externalise that, just for a moment…

The anger becomes sadness, bitterness.

And Rose Tico… Fanboys didn't like her in *The Last Jedi*, so when it came to *Rise of Skywalker*, she was as good as cut entirely.

5.2

The FIGURE *is projected on the door once more.*

FIGURE. She's a shit character.

JOE *turns to see the figure, then looks up at the tech box.*

JOE. Dylan… can we… can you… help!

No answer from Dylan…

FIGURE. You don't really like Rose Tico and the Canto Bight subplot.

JOE *turns back to the figure.*

JOE. Look – whoever you are – can you please just accept that we're allowed to like different things?! People can like *The Last Jedi* if they want to. They can like *The Phantom Menace* if they really want to!

FIGURE. Who's the protagonist?

JOE. What?

FIGURE. Who's the main character in *The Phantom Menace*?

JOE. Well, I guess Anakin –

FIGURE. Wrong! We don't meet Anakin till halfway through.

JOE. Obi Wan Kenobi?

FIGURE. Nope!

JOE. Padmé?

FIGURE. Come on, Joe, you're smarter than that.

JOE. Fine: tell me!

FIGURE. There is no protagonist. Which is one of many, many reasons why it's shit.

JOE *laughs*.

What?! Don't laugh at me!

JOE (*still laughing*). Sorry it's… how angry this makes you. They're just films!

FIGURE. They are NOT just films!

JOE. Okay.

FIGURE. They are SO much *more* than films!

JOE. Alright, sorry!

FIGURE. The only good ones are the originals. And even then, only one is a masterpiece.

JOE. Ah yes, of course: *Return of the Jedi*.

FIGURE. That better be a joke.

JOE. Obviously it's a joke… Everyone knows it's *The Holiday Special*.

FIGURE. That wasn't funny.

JOE. It was very funny. Wait… I do know who the protagonist is in *The Phantom Menace*!

FIGURE. No, you don't, there isn't one.

JOE. Yes, there is!

FIGURE. Who?!

JOE. Jar Jar Binks!

FIGURE. Fuck off!!

Blackout. Dramatic music.

The figure takes his hood down.

And we see that he is JOE, *aged fifty. Grey-white hair and beard. Dishevelled, unkempt, wearing the same dressing gown* JOE *is wearing onstage.*

JOE. Oh crap…

OLD JOE. So, now you know.

JOE. Oh *crap!*

OLD JOE. Not who you were expecting?

JOE. Not quite. You look really… grown up. How old are you?

OLD JOE. Fifty.

JOE. Eugh.

OLD JOE. What?

JOE. Nothing. So, I'm really going to turn into you?

OLD JOE. Perhaps… what do you think?

JOE. I could do worse. What's it like when I'm fifty?

OLD JOE. I thought you hated spoilers?

JOE. I do, but… okay don't tell me. Actually, just give me a hint.

OLD JOE. Okay… You're going to love it.

JOE. Really?!

OLD JOE. No! It's shit.

JOE. Oh. Tell me about the games.

OLD JOE. The technology's good. But the games are garbage.

JOE. Really? Why?

OLD JOE. No one has any new ideas. So all we get are remakes and reboots. And nothing's as good as the original.

JOE. That's annoying.

OLD JOE. It's really annoying.

JOE. And what about… you know, the world.

OLD JOE. You think things are bad there now, it's worse here.

JOE. Okay, don't tell me anything else, I don't want any more spoilers.

OLD JOE. Drought. Famine. War. Plague…

JOE. Yeah well, we kind of have that already, so –

OLD JOE (*bitter laugh*). That's a tutorial, by comparison.

Beat. JOE takes this in.

JOE. So… it's like the prequels?

OLD JOE. What?!

JOE. If this was *Star Wars* it'd be like me here now, is the prequels: democracy in peril but people pretending it's fine, then where you are, twenty years later it's the originals, and it's all a bit fucked, and you need a hero to come along and save the day.

OLD JOE (*like a Palpatine impression*). Young fool.

I'm not waiting for a hero, I'm taking control of my own destiny. And I think you've got your timelines confused.

JOE. Right, yeah so my *younger* self is the prequels, *I'm* the originals, and *you're* the… sequels?

OLD JOE. Don't you *dare* call me that!

JOE. Sorry.

OLD JOE. Your childhood was the original trilogy. That's all that was good.

JOE. That… can't be true.

OLD JOE. It is true.

JOE. Come on: *Revenge of the Sith* isn't *that* bad…

OLD JOE. Not *Star Wars*! My life. Your life. His life. You've always hoped it would get better. Yet it only gets worse. But you can change it.

JOE. Right… you said *perhaps* I'm going to turn into you… (*Laughs, realising something.*) Oh! I know what's happening here! Are you trying to show me three versions of myself – my past, my present, my future – so I change my ways? Are you trying to *Muppet Christmas Carol* me?

OLD JOE. Do you mean am I trying to *Christmas Carol* you?

JOE. No, I mean *Muppet Christmas Carol* me.

OLD JOE. The Muppets didn't write *A Christmas Carol*!

JOE. They might as well have.

OLD JOE *sighs with frustration.*

Alright – what is it you want me to change?

OLD JOE. Well, it won't work if I just tell you.

JOE. We haven't got long left so could you just tell me?

OLD JOE (*Palpatine laugh*). I can show you…

JOE. So – we're going to go to your time?!

OLD JOE. Sometimes you have to go backwards to go forwards. Sit.

JOE *collapses into the chair, as if not fully in control of his own body.*

JOE. Wait, aren't you like the Ghost of Fanboy Future? Why are you showing me a memory?

OLD JOE. You're hiding something from the audience.

JOE. I'm not hiding anything!

OLD JOE. About Gaia: there was, of course, another Christmas with her.

JOE. Please, no! I don't want to see that Christmas!

On both the door and the TV screen, corresponding footage of Michael Caine from The Muppet Christmas Carol. *We see videos that have played throughout the show – of* YOUNG JOE, *of the 1997 General Election, killer whales swimming, David Attenborough, rewinding. We see clips of many other films, games and moments of history* JOE *has referenced throughout the show, all rewinding at breakneck speed.*

No. Please I beg you. Stop. I can't go back there. Stop!

5.3

The video/projection cuts out, lights snap to a different state, jarringly cheerful instrumental Christmas music plays. We're somewhere else – a memory…

JOE. Is it because I'm too passive?

GAIA (*looking down at her hands*). No.

JOE. Too indecisive?

GAIA. No.

JOE. Am I too obsessive?

GAIA. You mean, right now?

JOE. No not right now, I can't help being obsessive right now. I mean in general?

GAIA. No. You're not too obsessive. You're not too anything. Or not enough of anything.

JOE. Then, I don't understand.

Beat. GAIA meets JOE's eyes.

GAIA. Do you remember in Iceland, after we saw the orcas? When we were driving and couldn't see the glacier?

JOE. Yeah…

GAIA. At the time, I thought I just couldn't see it from where we were.

But I realised, afterwards, it's because it's not there any more.

It's gone.

I should have noticed sooner, but I think I didn't want to believe it.

And I'm sorry it's gone and I'm sad it's gone and I wish it was still here. But I can't bring it back. And nor can you.

The memory fades. JOE is in darkness.

5.4

JOE *leaps up, yelling into the empty space* – OLD JOE *cannot be seen.*

JOE. Why did you show me that?! It happened. So what?! What is this truth? What do you want me to change?

Am I too obsessive?

Am I too passive?

Am I too weak?

OLD JOE *reappears, laughing.*

That's it, isn't it? That's what I need to change. I'm weak.

OLD JOE. Yes. And it all starts with him. With the youngling.

JOE *looks at the TV. The screen is empty.*

JOE. My younger self?

OLD JOE. You must spoil it for him.

JOE. Spoil what? You mean… the future?

OLD JOE. Yes… starting with… *The Phantom Menace.*

Beat.

JOE. Sorry?

OLD JOE. You heard me.

JOE. Spoil *The Phantom Menace*?!

OLD JOE. Tell him what happens in it. Explain exactly what's wrong with it, every shitty detail so he sees it for what it is, and hates it as much as I do.

JOE. How will that work?

OLD JOE. It just will.

JOE. Yeah but how?

OLD JOE. How does the Force work?

JOE. Midi-chlorians.

OLD JOE. Fuck off!

JOE. I don't understand, why do you want me to spoil *The Phantom Menace*?

Lights fade down. OLD JOE *becomes disembodied, a voice in the darkness. On both the TV screen and the door we see* YOUNG JOE *crying, raging, screaming, and then flickers of him matching* OLD JOE*'s composition, lighting and expression.*

OLD JOE. If you spoil it, he won't see it. He won't make those memories with Gaia, or Wayne, or Obi. He won't fall in love with the world. And he won't waste his time thinking he can save it. He's so pathetic, that spoiling that film will spoil everything else.

JOE. No, it won't. There's loads of other things he loves…

JOE *grabs the remote and presses a button.*

Donkey Kong Country!

On the TV screen: Donkey Kong running through the 'Jungle Hijinks' level.

OLD JOE. Overrated!

On the TV screen: Donkey Kong dies.

JOE. Birdwatching!

On the TV screen: a rare parrot in its habitat.

OLD JOE. Laughable!

On the TV screen: the rare parrot attacks the camera operator.

JOE. David Attenborough!

On the TV screen: David Attenborough on a beautiful beach, narrating.

OLD JOE. Tragic, old fool!

On the TV screen: David Attenborough looks tired and sad.

JOE. Killer whales!

On the TV screen: orcas swimming gracefully.

OLD JOE. They're all extinct now.

On the TV screen: beached orcas, slowly suffocating.

JOE. No! They can't be.

OLD JOE. See? If you knew this twenty years ago you wouldn't be in pain right now. You'd just be angry. And you'd be strong.

JOE. Why should I do what you tell me?

OLD JOE *holds up the Jar Jar Sticky Tongue Toy.*

OLD JOE. Remember this?

JOE. Hey, that's mine… what are you –

OLD JOE. Do it – now!

OLD JOE *holds a pair of* Warhammer *clippers, threatening to cut the tongue off the toy.*

JOE (*defiant*). No!

OLD JOE *cuts off Jar Jar's tongue.*

Wait no stop… Nooooo!

JOE *falls to his knees.* OLD JOE *laughs like Palpatine once more.*

FUCK OFF!

OLD JOE *vanishes. Lights up suddenly.* JOE *looks around.* OLD JOE *is gone.*

JOE *is furious, lost, alone.*

5.5

YOUNG JOE *appears on the screen.*

YOUNG JOE. Please tell me!

JOE *looks up. He's not in the mood for this now.*

JOE. About what?

YOUNG JOE. *Episode I: The Phantom Menace.*

JOE. No.

YOUNG JOE. Pleeeeease!

JOE. No.

YOUNG JOE. I want to know what happens. In the film. And in the future!

JOE *is fighting something within himself.*

JOE. Well… I'm not telling you.

YOUNG JOE. Why not?

JOE. I… I'm tired.

YOUNG JOE. Aww, that's no fun.

JOE. You're a kid: go play something. Watch something. Go have fun.

YOUNG JOE. But I want to know what it's like!

JOE. No, you don't.

YOUNG JOE. I do!

JOE. No, you really don't.

YOUNG JOE. I want to know *everythiiiiing*!

JOE. And I want you to go. I want to you to shut up and leave me alone. Fuck off.

YOUNG JOE. I hate you!

JOE. I know.

YOUNG JOE. Well, take care of yourself, Joe. I guess that's what you're best at.

YOUNG JOE *storms off, leaving the empty background of the garden fence.*

5.6

JOE *turns to us once more, realising something for the first time.*

JOE. I'm jealous of him. I want what he has. I want to go back there. But I can't.

I can do the next best thing. I can tell him everything. Destroy what he has, so I don't feel like this any more. I want...

The orcas to die, their bloated bodies stranded, one by one, till every last beach is rotting with their corpses. I want...

To erase my save files, tear up my books, throw my films and games into toxic, plastic bonfire. I want...

To tell him everything. If he really wants to know what he's like when he's thirty – spoiler alert: he's pathetic. He's weak. That's what he becomes. He shouts from the sidelines but never gets involved, he sits inside, watching the same films, playing the same games, hiding from the truth that the world he thought he could save, the person he thought he could be, is a stupid fantasy.

I want to tell him that the world is dying.

That there's nothing he can do.

And it doesn't matter.

Because I fucking hate it.

5.7

JOE *moves to the TV screen and grabs the remote.* OLD JOE *reappears.*

OLD JOE. Are you ready?

JOE. Yes.

OLD JOE. Good!

> JOE *rewinds the tape to:*

YOUNG JOE. Please tell me! (*The tape skips.*)... *Episode I: The Phantom Menace!* (*The tape skips.*)... I want to know *everything.*

> JOE *pauses the tape. He hesitates.*

OLD JOE. Do it! Embrace your hatred. Your anger.

> JOE *presses play, so* YOUNG JOE *is listening.*

JOE (*to* YOUNG JOE). Okay, I'll tell you. What happens in *The Phantom Menace* is –

> *The tape starts skipping.* JOE *tries to regain control, rewinding it back to the same place.*

YOUNG JOE. I want to know *everything*!

JOE. Right, what happens is –

> *The tape skips again,* JOE *rewinds it back to the same place and presses play again.*

YOUNG JOE. ...*everything*!

JOE. Just still stay still and I'll tell you.

> *The tape skips again, fast-forwarding, rewinding.*

Hey, come back! Come back!

> *But the tape won't behave.* JOE *smacks the remote and tries to regain control but it's not working. On the TV screen,* YOUNG JOE *is running around, having fun, enjoying his childhood. Alone.*

> *Birdwatching.*

> *Playing* Donkey Kong Country.

Watching Star Wars.

Swinging a lightsaber around.

We linger on YOUNG JOE *in his Superman costume, swinging the Jar Jar Sticky Tongue Toy by the tongue.*

JOE *watches it all, then calls out to* OLD JOE*:*

JOE. I can't do this.

OLD JOE. What?

JOE. I can't spoil it for him. He's going to like that film. *I* liked that film. I still like it.

OLD JOE. Say that again.

JOE. I still like it. I still like *The Phantom Menace*.

OLD JOE. Liar!

JOE. I'm not lying. It's true.

OLD JOE. Name one thing you like about it?!

JOE. The score – 'Dual of the Fates' – absolute masterpiece!

OLD JOE. Fine. I'll allow that. But only that.

JOE. The lightsaber fight.

OLD JOE. Well-choreographed, but it's too little, too late.

JOE. The podracing!

OLD JOE. It's irrelevant. It's just for fun.

JOE. It's supposed to be fun! I think young Obi Wan's cool, I think Padmé's awesome. I love Palpatine's deception.

OLD JOE. Stop…

OLD JOE *flickers.*

JOE. I like the politics – it's not perfect but it's ambitious and I love what it's trying to say about the world.

OLD JOE. Stop!

OLD JOE *flickers, damaged, burning… in trouble!*

JOE. I love the environmental theme – the Jedi rallying the Gungans to save their planet.

OLD JOE. STOP!!!

OLD JOE *flickers some more.*

JOE. And you know what else I love?

OLD JOE. Don't! Don't you dare!

JOE. I love Jar Jar Binks!

OLD JOE *flickers even more.*

OLD JOE. NOOOOOOOOOOOOOOOOOOO!!!

OLD JOE *starts to disintegrate.*

He vanishes.

Silence.

5.8

JOE *picks up the toy, blue lightsaber he had at the start of the show.*

JOE. I don't want to ruin my childhood.

I *want* my childhood.

JOE *leaves the stage.*

On both the TV screen and the door, we see YOUNG JOE, *in his Superman costume. He draws a red lightsaber.*

YOUNG JOE. I've been waiting for you, Joe, for a long time. Finally, we meet once more.

The video/projection pans to reveal JOE, *on screen, hood up, blue lightsaber drawn.*

When you left me, I was merely learning. But now – I'm a master!

JOE. Only a master of mischief, Joe!

They play-fight with their toy lightsabers.

JOE and YOUNG JOE *run around, having fun, enjoying their childhood.*

Birdwatching.

Playing Donkey Kong Country.

Watching Star Wars.

Together.

JOE *is standing on a chair.*

JOE. It's over, Joe. I've got the high ground.

YOUNG JOE. You've underestimated my abilities!

They fight with the toy lightsabers again.

You've grown weak, old man!

JOE. If you cut me down, I will grow stronger than you could even imagine.

They fight some more.

JOE *lifts his lightsaber up, closes his eyes* (*like Obi Wan in* A New Hope).

YOUNG JOE *smacks* JOE *with the lightsaber.*

JOE *vanishes – his dressing gown, then his lightsaber, fall to the ground.* YOUNG JOE *looks around.*

Lights up onstage.

JOE *reappears onstage, no longer in his dressing gown.*

He turns to the TV.

Now… go!

YOUNG JOE. No! I can't leave you – I need to save you.

JOE. You have…

5.9

JOE *looks at the audience. Then back at the TV.* YOUNG JOE *is gone again.*

JOE. I have to stop living in the past. Gaia, Wayne and Obi aren't in my life any more.

Those times are gone.

But I wouldn't change it. That boy has all of it to look forward to.

YOUNG JOE *reappears on the screen.*

YOUNG JOE. You really hate spoilers, don't you?

JOE. You don't need me to tell you your future. If anything, I should be learning from you.

YOUNG JOE. Is that a… compliment?

JOE (*smiles*). Yeah. No one can save the world on their own. But I want to find a way to help. I want to try and put something good into it. And I think that starts with looking after you more.

YOUNG JOE *stares blankly.*

YOUNG JOE. I don't really know what you're talking about…

JOE. Don't worry about it right now.

YOUNG JOE. Okay. So… I'm really going to turn into you?

JOE. Afraid so. What do you think?

YOUNG JOE *considers for a moment, then shrugs.*

YOUNG JOE. I could do worse.

Beat.

Can you tell me one thing though?!

JOE. What?

YOUNG JOE. How do I do the ninety-nine-lives trick on *Donkey Kong Country*?

JOE. Go to the file select screen. Press down, Y, down, down Y.

YOUNG JOE. Oh!

JOE. Just be careful you don't accidentally erase your save file in the process.

YOUNG JOE. Okay.

JOE. Seriously, don't mess around with that.

YOUNG JOE. Don't worry, I won't.

JOE. Are you going to play it now?

YOUNG JOE. No.

> YOUNG JOE *hold up his binoculars and notepad.*

> I'm going birdwatching!

> YOUNG JOE *leaves the screen again, leaving the empty garden behind him.*

JOE. Alright. See you later then.

> *Beat.*

> YOUNG JOE *reappears.*

YOUNG JOE. Joe?

> JOE *looks at the TV.*

> YOUNG JOE *holds up the Jar Jar Sticky Tongue Toy.*

> Take care of yourself.

> YOUNG JOE *throws the Jar Jar Sticky Tongue Toy beyond the camera.*

> JOE, *onstage, catches it.*

> YOUNG JOE *waves and leaves the screen.*

> JOE *looks at the toy.*

Epilogue

JOE. Your younger self is with you, like it or not. And you can hate them. Or you can love them.

I spent too long ignoring mine. Looking for heroes in the wrong places. Being angry about the wrong things.

I can't unmelt a glacier. Or turn someone away from the dark side. Or reach someone who's gone.

(*Glancing briefly over his shoulder at the TV.*) But I want to find the joy and hope he had, so I can put my anger somewhere useful.

I want to go out into the world.

JOE *places the Jar Jar Sticky Tongue Toy on top of the TV.*

And I want to remember that

– however frightening it can be –

I still fucking love it.

Lights down.

The TV winks out.

Blackout.

End of play.

FIVE YEARS WITH THE WHITE MAN

Eloka Obi and Saul Boyer

*For those that have been and are being made to feel that they
don't belong in Britain. May we continue to witness a change
towards an equal society.*

E.O.

*For my parents, Lucille Dweck and Martin Boyer, who fostered
in me the fire of creativity and the will to sustain it, and for my
Grandmother, Suzy Dweck, whose expulsion from her home in
North Africa seemed not to diminish her life spirit,
but to galvanise it.*

S.B.

ELOKA OBI

Eloka Obi is a Nigerian-British writer. *Five Years with the White Man* is Eloka's first play. He is currently developing his own TV series with a major broadcaster.

SAUL BOYER

Saul Boyer is a writer and performer, trained at ArtsEd, the National Youth Theatre, and Cambridge University. He is also the co-Artistic Director of Unleash the Llama.

Saul's solo-show, *Man of One Hundred Faces*, completed a sell-out run at the 2022 Edinburgh Festival Fringe and the King's Head Theatre. It was listed in the *Guardian*'s 'Readers' Favourite Stage Shows of 2022': 'A magical drama. Proper storytelling by a virtuoso performer.' He performed and co-wrote *JEW…ish* – described as 'delectable… and explosive' (*Broadway World*) – at the Edinburgh Festival Fringe (2019), the King's Head Theatre (2020) and KHT Online (2021), where it had sell-out runs. Alongside stage productions, Saul continues to write for television and film. As a performer, Saul has recently appeared in *Murderabilia* (Audible), *Pseudocide* (Spotify), *Bad Women: The Ripper Retold* (Pushkin), and *Alone* by Moray Hunter (Radio 4). Saul is represented by Sarah Williams at Independent Talent.

SAM RAYNER
Director and Dramaturg

Sam Rayner is a director, movement director and dramaturg. He trained at Cambridge University and l'École Internationale de Théâtre Jacques Lecoq. He is committed to creating accessible and diverse work that uses physicality to inspire the imagination.

His directing credits include an acrobatic staging of *Serse* for Opera Holland Park ('fantastically detailed', *Guardian*); *Man of One Hundred Faces* – exploring espionage in Revolutionary Russia – listed in the *Guardian*'s 'Readers' Favourite Stage Shows of 2022' (Edinburgh Fringe/King's Head Theatre); and co-directing *The Man Who Thought He Knew Too Much* (Edinburgh Fringe/UK and international tour) – 'physical theatre at its most immaculate' (*The Scotsman*).

Sam is a co-Artistic Director of the multi-award-winning international physical-theatre company Voloz Collective and a co-founder of Unleash the Llama.

His movement direction credits include *Jack Whitehall: At Large* (Hammersmith Apollo/UK Tour/NETFLIX); *Leo Reich: Literally Who Cares?!* (Soho Theatre/Pleasance Courtyard) – listed as the *Guardian*'s 'Best Comedy Show of 2022'; and *Jordan Brookes: BLEED* (Soho Theatre/Pleasance Courtyard), described as 'a fearless display of physicality' (The List).

His credits as Associate Director include *Broken Wings* (Theatre Royal Haymarket/Dubai Opera/Katara Opera) and *Umm Kulthum and the Golden Era* (London Palladium/Dubai Opera).

Five Years with the White Man was first performed at VAULT Festival on 28 February 2023, presented by Unleash the Llama. The cast was as follows:

A. B. C. MERRIMAN-LABOR/DUMEBI	Joseph Akubeze

Concept by	Eloka Obi, Saul Boyer and Sam Rayner
Written by	Eloka Obi and Saul Boyer
Director & Dramaturg	Sam Rayner
Associate Director	Nebiu Samuel
Producer	Unleash the Llama

The play was previously performed as a rehearsed reading at Sands Films Studios in Rotherhithe, with the support of Lung Theatre, on 22 March 2022. The company was as above.

The play was workshopped at The Brick, London, and London Performance Studios in January 2022 with Theo St. Claire playing A. B. C. Merriman-Labor/Dumebi and Frederick Waxman as the sound designer.

Acknowledgements

With our enormous gratitude to Professor Joseph J. Bangura, Danell Jones, Melbourne Garber and Shenagh Cameron – for their scholarship, generosity, guidance and humour.

'It has been said that mine is a humorous style... I shall be sorry to be regarded solely as a humourist, for one of my aims in writing is not so much to be humorous, as to reveal such truths as may be best spoken in jests... I am of the opinion that the world will be better prepared to hear me if I come in the guise of a jester.'

A. B. C. Merriman-Labor,
Britons Through Negro Spectacles, *1909*

Characters

AUGUSTUS BOYLE CHAMBERLAYNE MERRIMAN-
LABOR, *an incorrigible believer*
JIM, *Augustus's devout uncle*
GILLIAN, *a devoted teacher and Augustus's mother*
JOHNNY, *a Christian merchant from Freetown*
GWAKI WA, *a Mende Muslim meat-merchant*
FATHER, *an irascible businessman*
THE MOB, *a spokesperson for the townspeople of Waterloo,
Sierra Leone*
DUMEBI, *Alfred's partner, not an actor*
GRANDFATHER, *Augustus's surrogate parent and educator*
A reluctant TECHNICIAN
ALFRED, *Dumebi's late partner, the author of the show, an
academic and idealist*
IJEOMA, *Dumebi's mother, who allowed her son to Trick or
Treat*
ADIATU, *Alfred's mother*
A musical MILKMAN
COACHMAN, *a conversational cabby*
LANDLADY, *an economical businesswoman*
JOHN, *a childhood friend, confidant, and partner*
ANNOUNCER, *a showman*
JASON, *a friend from Freetown, in unfamiliar circumstances*
FACTORY OWNER, *a reluctant investor in the African
General Agency*
ZIPPORAH, *John's trusting fiancée*
JC COLE, *Zipporah's father, a Sierra Leonean businessman*
POLICE OFFICER, *a bobby on the beat*
JUDGE 1 & 2, *two benchers of Lincoln's Inn*
A downtrodden, if bigoted, BEGGAR
MARY, *John's mother*
DEPUTY GOVERNOR, *the colonial authority in Zungeru*

Note

With the exception of Alfred, whose voice should be (at least in part) recorded in performance, and the Technician, whose lines should be delivered by the technician operating during the performance, all parts are to be played by one performer.

Words in [square brackets] are unspoken.

Scene One – The Lecture

Darkness. Silence.

Suddenly, a match strikes. The flickering light illuminates a face.

Lights up to reveal a lecture theatre, complete with Edwardian furnishings and accoutrements – including a globe, desk, and podium.

Music plays: 'Symphonic Variations on an African Air' by Samuel Coleridge-Taylor.

AUGUSTUS BOYLE CHAMBERLAYNE MERRIMAN-LABOR. Welcome, ladies and gentlemen, fellow countrymen, friends, to my modest little lecture.

Take my arm, traveller, and together we shall penetrate into the deepest depths of depravity! Together we shall trudge towards a terrible truth wrapped in malevolent mystery!

Our spine-chilling subject…?

Whoosh. With one pull of a cord, a curtain springs open, exposing a poster mounted on the lecture podium. It reads: 'Five Years With The White Man'.

AUGUSTUS *registers the audience's reaction.*

Yes, you may laugh! I have long been persuaded that the world only listens to truth if it is spoken in jest. Though I am no jester.

For five long years, I sojourned in the horrifying heart of whiteness: London! This is what I saw…

But I must warn you, before you go on, if you are of a nervous disposition, leave now, for your eyes may never unsee, nor your ears unhear the terrifying tale my tongue must tell.

He gestures for the audience to leave.

No?

Good.

Very good.

But remember, you entered with your eyes open!

He moves in front of the podium.

To begin, at the beginning.

We are transported to AUGUSTUS*'s childhood home in Waterloo, Sierra Leone.*

My name is Augustus Boyle Chamberlayne Merriman-Labor – and I am a naughty little boy.

He cries loudly into the air – and tears around the stage. Then stops abruptly and looks at the audience.

At all hours, be it morning, noon or night, I bellow as loud as my little lungs will allow – and there's nothing anyone can do to stop me!

It is my Uncle Jim who wakes up first.

JIM. Gillian!

AUGUSTUS. He's studying to become a minister of the church – but I push his faith to the limit.

JIM. It's four o'clock in the morning! What the hell is wrong with your boy?

GILLIAN. He's just… expressing himself.

AUGUSTUS *lets out another bellow, even louder and more absurd.*

GILLIAN *laughs at this preposterous outburst.*

(*To* AUGUSTUS *now.*) One day he will become a great speaker! And an even greater writer – hm? Just like Daddy! Remember, my son, inexhaustible power surges within you!

AUGUSTUS. Inexhaustible power surges within me!

(*To the audience.*) I am little more than a toddler, but already I know my voice must be heard.

I spend most of my days waiting, until it is time for my friend John to come over to play. He's a strange child – who prefers to play with the dogs in the street than the other boys at school.

Nevertheless, we compete to see who can bellow the loudest. I always win!

He demonstrates.

Father's too busy writing in his office to discipline me. So my mother is left with no choice –

GILLIAN *yells!*

GILLIAN. The White Man is coming! The White Man will come and take you away!

AUGUSTUS *mimes 'Shhhh' – wide-eyed with mock fear.*

AUGUSTUS. All across Africa small children are disciplined with the same cry. But it stopped me in my tracks. I was terrified. But also… curious.

We are transported to the marketplace. We might hear occasional cries of 'Cassava, get your cassava!' or the lowing of cattle.

Market day. My mother hunts for bargains, while I am left with two meat merchants: Johnny Taylor, a Christian from Freetown, and Gwaki Wa, a Mende Muslim from the north. I gather all my gumption and ask –

Does the White Man exist?

JOHNNY. What you say, little man?

AUGUSTUS. The White Man?

JOHNNY. What about him?

AUGUSTUS. Does he exist?

JOHNNY. What do you think, Gwaki Wa? Does the White Man exist?

GWAKI WA. Oh yes… a terrifying creature with horns and long pointy teeth and eyes the size of your hands.

JOHNNY. You'll scare the boy!

AUGUSTUS. I'm not scared! Where does he come from?

JOHNNY. Well, if you read Darwin, you cannot deny that all humans are descended from a certain species of simian…

GWAKI WA. No, sir. Don't let Johnny fool you. The forefather of the colonial oppressor cannot be anything as manlike as the simian. The original ancestor of the White must be the filthy pig.

GWAKI WA chops the meat and stares at AUGUSTUS sternly.

And pork, as you may know, is haram!

He erupts into laughter.

AUGUSTUS. They laugh. I laugh. We all laugh.

Now whenever my mother uses the White Bogey Man to scare me to school and to shock me to sleep and so forth, I laugh!

He tears around the stage shouting again.

I don't give a damn about this kidnapping white somebody who seems to be a little like the last judgement: always coming, coming, coming, but never actually arriving!

He continues to tear around the stage shouting. Even louder. Until suddenly – he stops dead, listening intently.

Until two years later.

A flash of lightning. In the dark, we catch a momentary glimpse of the fabled 'White Man' that GWAKI WA described: a terrifying, wraith-like creature, complete with horns and teeth filed to violent points. Then, we are transported back to Augustus's childhood home.

My father shakes me awake in the middle of the night.

FATHER. Pack everything, boy! They are coming.

AUGUSTUS. Our home in the town of Waterloo, Sierra Leone, is surrounded.

Villagers with torches and pitchforks are battering down the door. My father pushes me through a hole in the wall, into the back garden, murmuring…

FATHER. It's my fault. It's my fault.

The sound of a loud thump at the door.

AUGUSTUS. He had published an article exposing the rampant corruption of the imperial government: names, dates, crimes.

He holds up a newspaper.

He called the piece 'Three Years: What I Saw' – but in this colony of ours, it was better to play blind.

THE MOB. Look at where your writing gets you, Joshua! Next time keep your mouth shut!

A roar erupts from the mob. The house is set alight.

DUMEBI*'s phone bleeps.*

Scene Two – The Email

DUMEBI (*to the audience*). *Sorry, sorry.*

He reads an email.

(*Pointing up to the tech box.*) Did you get this just now?

(*To the audience.*) Wait, sorry, sorry – one second.

(*To the tech box.*) The email? Here, were you not CCd, no? It says:

'Dear Dumebi – "Doemebee…"' spelt wrong.

'Thank you very much for submitting your play to our theatre.

Unfortunately, only a small percentage of new writing can make it through to the stage, and sadly your submission has been unsuccessful on this occasion.

We know how much effort goes into writing, and we appreciate you taking the time to apply. The quality of scripts submitted is really high, and we want to encourage you to keep telling your stories, and to look out for future development opportunities. Thank you again for letting us read your work and all the very best.

All the best.'

(*To the audience.*) Four months to send that email?

(*To the tech box.*) Pisstake, man… absolutely.

(*To the audience*.) Sorry, sorry, basically… nah, basically…
you see… well, I've broken the illusion now.

He waves his phone.

So my name is Alfred… no sorry, what? My name is Dumebi.

I would like to start by saying I am not an actor – okay? –
clearly, not an actor.

My boyfriend, who is called Alfred – Basically, he's an
academic, like a historian.

Looking at a specific member of the audience.

Wow, you look so disappointed – not what you paid for.

DUMEBI *laughs*.

No, look he studied History at Cambridge and he's basically
scarily obsessed with this Black guy from the nineteenth
century – Augustus Boyle Chamberlayne Merriman-Labor.
Yeah, I know. It's a lot.

Anyway, yeah, he wrote, well he started writing this play
Five Years with the White Man – it was the name of one of
Augustus's lectures, and yeah, Alfred wrote… a… was
writing a play about Augustus.

But, yeah he ummm… he worships history, Alfred does.

For context, me and Alfred started dating in 2017 – roughly
five years ago, hence '*Five Years with the White Man*'.

DUMEBI *laughs to himself.*

Nah, I'm joking, that's not even funny.

He looks back at the specific audience member.

Ooh, really disappointed.

It's a coincidence that we started dating five years ago.
Alfred is actually Black. Was Black – nah, I can't say 'was'
there, can I? Because even though he's… but then people do
say 'he was a historian' or 'he was a renowned academic' but
I dunno saying 'he was Black' sounds a bit strange, no?

Wow, for more context, Alfred is dead.

I'm doing this for him, I'm not an actor. But, sorry to stop the
performance, I just keep getting these emails, it's incessant.

No one would pick this up.

(*To the tech box*.) Probably shouldn't say that?

No, no, it's going to be good, it's gonna be good.

(*To the audience*.) Sorry for stopping.

Also, I'm not alone, might as well introduce [insert name of technician].

He points to the tech box

(*To the tech box*.) Go on, say hi [name].

The TECHNICIAN *embarrassingly acknowledges the audience somehow.*

[*He/she/they*] are actually a technician.

I should say, not that Alfred was boring, he wasn't, he's great, but I have added in bits. I mean, I'm not a writer either but yeah, I read this book: *The Art of Dramatic Writing*, and I've added bits, unless it's just a history lesson.

Scene Three – Leaving to London

Soundscape of the burning home.

AUGUSTUS. My father's words had cost us everything: our home, our friends, my mother.

She left on a boat, bound for 'a better place'.

As tears ran down my father's cheeks on that dock, he vowed that I would not end up like him.

He understood the power of books. He just didn't want his son to write them.

FATHER. Stop showing off. Do something with your life. Be practical.

AUGUSTUS. But I had grown used to bellowing.

I unleash my anger on the one who is closest to me: John.

AUGUSTUS *launches himself at* JOHN. *As they fight, their boyish 'bellowing' transforms into the vocalised frustration of young men locked in a tussle.*

We fight. I always win.

JOHN *is pinned to the ground. A beat. It lasts too long.*

A door opens. Both their heads turn, as if 'caught' in the act.

It's not allowed to continue.

FATHER. Boy! You will learn the hard way.

AUGUSTUS. My father sends me to live with my grandfather.

But far from crushing my dreams, the old man merely intensifies them.

GRANDFATHER. Your mother tells me, you want to be the greatest writer in the empire.

AUGUSTUS (*wiping away tears*). Yes, sir. I want to go to London!

GRANDFATHER. Then go to London you shall!

AUGUSTUS. He teaches me everything I know. Latin, history, literature, theology…

All topics… all except one.

(*To his* GRANDFATHER.) Grandfather – how come everything is white?

GRANDFATHER. What do you say, my dear boy?

AUGUSTUS. Jesus? The angels? The Archbishop of Canterbury? When we die will we go to heaven?

GRANDFATHER. Naturally we go to heaven.

AUGUSTUS. Then what happened to all the Black angels when they made the pictures?

GRANDFATHER. Be quiet with all your foolishness!

AUGUSTUS. But I couldn't – the question disturbed me.

(*To* GRANDFATHER.) Why is everything bad black? The black sheep's an outcast, black cats are bad luck, if I threaten you I blackmail you – why don't they call it white-mail? They lie too!

GRANDFATHER. Grow up!

AUGUSTUS. I do. I work hard. Graduate top of my class. Make a name for myself in Freetown. And now, a decade later – I stand on the dock. In one hand: a letter of admission to the London Society of Authors; in the other, a letter of enrolment in The Inns of Court. Father had agreed to sponsor my trip, so long as I used the opportunity to train in London as a barrister. But, as I watch the waves crashing onto the shore, I can't help but think, my own story is yet to be written.

We hear the sound of the surf, crashing waves and a foghorn.

On the sea breeze I smell my mother's scent, the rushing waves speak with her voice: 'write always…'

He makes the gesture of her wave.

It is time. I steel myself, and step up into the future –

FATHER. Augustus!

AUGUSTUS. But a voice holds me back. That hat. That swagger. My father.

FATHER. Augustus! I'm giving you six months to make something of yourself, and I expect results. I need contacts for Labor, Labor and Co.

AUGUSTUS. The family business…

FATHER. Make sure you sell some furniture – become a barrister and return in triumph! Then we will talk about writing!

AUGUSTUS *goes to board the boat, but his* FATHER *holds him back.*

Don't think you can do it by yourself. No one there cares – the White Man cannot help you! He is too busy helping himself.

AUGUSTUS *goes to board the boat again, but again his* FATHER *holds him back.*

Don't forget who you are, or why you are there! Stay focused on *our* goals…

A beat. He's done now, surely… AUGUSTUS *goes to board the boat again, but again his* FATHER *stops him.*

…and stay away from their women!

AUGUSTUS (*with earnest gravity*). That won't be a problem.

He hands me a brown package.

FATHER. Open it when you're on deck.

AUGUSTUS. He marches off the jetty without another look back. But in my mind's eye, I see my mother waving from the wharf until the bay is a speck in the great blue.

We hear the boat's departure.

I open the package as Freetown flies into the distance and the engines sing. Nestled in the paper is a triple-ply, thick tweed suit.

He imagines strutting down a catwalk, admiring his reflection in the iron belly of the beast.

I feel something in the pocket. A leather wallet, containing one hundred pounds.

I laugh so loud, it ruffles the rats out of their place in the girders.

During the following dialogue, the soundscape slowly warps to become nightmarish. The sound of sea spray becomes a whisper above the growl of the ocean.

Looking out across the sea, as the sky goes dark, I fall asleep. I dream of my past. Of John. I had not seen him in so long. Now I may never see him again.

The sound of a foghorn. A cry… 'LAND HOOOOOO!'

I wake with a jolt –

He hits his head on the low ceiling.

…and rush to the bow. I can see it on the horizon. London is my future.

Foghorn. They arrive.

I had sought a land of peace and industry. I found chaos.

Silence. Too long. A beat has been missed. It's clear the actor has forgotten their lines.

Scene Four – Cassell House

DUMEBI. For fuck's sake.

Fuck.

Sorry, sorry.

DUMEBI *goes to pick up the script.*

Wow. Sorry.

DUMEBI *flicks through the script, confused.*

(*To the tech box.*) [Name], how much was this?

TECHNICIAN. [Says the ticket price.]

DUMEBI. What? I mean, I really tried, but I just couldn't afford an actor, obviously I should have, instead of me forgetting the lines.

Alfred never let me read this when he was alive. He'd always hide it from me, like it was his great work of art.

The following dialogue from ALFRED *may be pre-recorded and played, or performed by* DUMEBI.

ALFRED. When I'm finished you'll be the first to read it.

DUMEBI. Big man, you're not actually a playwright you know.

ALFRED.... Thank you. And you think I'm going to let you read it.

DUMEBI. Only joking! My likkle Shakey-speare.

ALFRED *and* DUMEBI *laugh together, until* DUMEBI *is left laughing alone – remembering how they laughed.*

When I did eventually read it, he was dead. 'Awww moment' – no, I mean technically I'm going against his will because he never finished. It's weird though because I read it and there were so many... parallels. Scary similarities that made me think that I should do this. The optimistic academic, obsessed with history and literature, from Sierra Leone, surrounded by cynics. And yeah, I mean, that's why I'm here. It's all quite... mad.

I'm not gonna lie, I'm not big on history and so, yeah I think... I dunno... I thought there'd maybe be bits where I just...

He gestures performatively with his hands.

I just tell you about me and Alfred.

He looks immediately at his hands, questioning why he did that.

Sorry. Okay? Okay.

Ummm. So I grew up on Cassell House estate opposite Stockwell Tube Station. We were flat thirty-three. I grew up with both parents, both Nigerian, but hey Nigerian parents with a little nuance – no one-dimensional mum with them 'ee-ees' and 'oo-oos' – no, we're not doing that today.

So, it was me, my mum, Ijeoma, my dad, Joseph, and my little sister, Uju – we were happy, it was cute, wholesome.

My parents are cool, you know. I swear we were like the only Black kids that got to Trick or Treat in the whole of South London.

Alfred and his mum, Adiatu, moved to number twenty-seven autumn 19… 1996. They moved in, and Mum felt the need to look after Adiatu. I think something happened with Alfred's dad but till this day I don't really know what happened there. Fathers!

Adiatu quickly became Aunty Adiatu, and by that Christmas, Mum was referring to her as her sister and the only time they would deny siblingship was every other Sunday when the Battle of Who Does West Africa's Iconic Rice Dish Best ensued. Aunty Adi and Alfred are Sierra Leonean, like Augustus.

IJEOMA. Our own is better!

ADIATU. Our own is better!

DUMEBI. It wasn't till the 2014 Jollofgate when Jamie Oliver succeeded in uniting Nigerians, Sierra Leoneans and all Africans with his sacrilegious attempt at jollof rice that my mum and Aunty Adi stopped fighting.

IJEOMA. Wetin be co-ri-ander inside d' rice?

ADIATU. Since when does it include cherry tomato?

DUMEBI. For a brief moment, both women put aside their conflict for a unified stance against what they saw… as an abomination.

My mum would force me to hang out with Alfred, and look after him, because he'd had a tough time…

Silence.

YOUNG DUMEBI (*to* YOUNG ALFRED). Are you okay?

What's wrong? Can you not speak?

Silence.

DUMEBI. It was weirdly beautiful when Alfred cried, he was always silent, face still. I remember so vividly the first time I saw it.

DUMEBI *stands awkwardly watching a crying* ALFRED. *He stares, unsure of what to do, and then slowly moves towards him and embraces him.* DUMEBI *pulls away.*

YOUNG DUMEBI. Do you wanna get a KitKat?

ALFRED *wipes his tears and nods.*

DUMEBI. I feel like it's human nature to constantly change our memories but I think, I think I can remember walking in complete silence to the shop and back, but you know when you're silent and it's not awkward, it's peaceful. Obviously I'm a kid, I didn't know that that was what it was, but it was that, you know, I'm not sure that makes sense – but, yeah, we felt close.

We bonded over our love for KitKats and our disinterest in Arsenal FC… *Gays.*

We got quite close. It feels silly saying we 'weren't like the other boys' on the estate but we actually weren't. His mum had this copy of the Aaliyah *One in a Million* album, which was shit-hot then, still is, and yeah, we'd listen on loop.

During this Aaliyah's 'One in a Million' plays.

Gosh we've always been gay, even before we knew it – every time 'Hot Like Fire' would end and the 'love it babe' intro for 'One in a Million' would start we would lie on the floor like Aaliyah on that car in the video, belting out –

He speaks/sings the chorus from 'One in a Million'.

DUMEBI *laughs and relives this memory. He's a bit emotional, but continues.*

Alfred and Aunty Adi moved to Bristol after a while. But, yeah we kind of lost contact, we drifted apart – Alfred got some scholarship at a school down there, went to Cambridge, got his bag. He always knew book that boy!

Scene Five – Year One

DUMEBI *takes a puff on his vape. Suddenly the stage is enveloped in mist.*

AUGUSTUS. I stepped off the dock with a fresh sense of purpose, my father's words ringing in my ears: become a barrister, return in triumph!

He begins to struggle through the mist.

London spread its arms cold and wide to receive its prodigal son.

He coughs and splutters.

I found myself bellower in the land of bellowers.

My favourite was the milkman...

MILKMAN. Milk eeeh! Milk oooh!

AUGUSTUS. I had thirty minutes to arrive at Lincoln's Inn for my matriculation!

I hailed a cab. Dodged the Punch and Judy man and the wailing sisters – and launched myself inside!

AUGUSTUS *climbs into the cab.*

COACHMAN. Don't mind the fog, sir. All over. Regrettable. Not like your country, I'm sure. Your provenance, sir? Where from? Where, original like? Oooh, Sierra Leone! Ooooooh exotic.

AUGUSTUS. As he babbled like a one-man Babel, my pen flashed in my notebook. Little did this coachman know, his charming idiocy would soon be immortalised forever in my satire of London life. Glimpses of London's glorious sights flashed through the window as I envisaged my meteoric rise to the immortal pantheon of English letters, between Chaucer and Shakespeare – Merriman-Labor! Oh merciful God, let it be thus!

AUGUSTUS *watches the landmarks pass outside the cab window.*

Westminster Cathedral! Home of Faith! The Bank of England! Home of Commerce!

Lincoln's Inn!

The cab stops. AUGUSTUS *gets out.*

I looked up at the home of British justice. I would take my place there as a student upon the morrow, for my father, for my grandfather, for my sponsors… and for myself. After all, reputation is the key to publication!

He writes this down in a pocket book.

Mmmm, reputation is the key to publication!

But reputation did not come cheap – nor did justice!

(*To an official.*) How much? Two hundred and fifty pounds, per year?

Certainly, certainly… well, here's fifty for now… and the rest will come… shortly. Good day. Sir…

The official wipes his hand on his jacket in disgust after shaking AUGUSTUS*'s hand.*

Then there was the little matter of accommodation… as an aspiring man of letters, I knew of no better residence than Bloomsbury!

(*Repeating to himself.*) Inexhaustible power surges within me, inexhaustible power surges within me, inexhaustible…

AUGUSTUS *knocks on a door.*

Good morning, sir – I'm looking for…

Door slams.

Any rooms avail–

Another door slams.

I'll pay up-front –

Another door slams.

Before you close the –

Another door slams.

I grew desperate. I had no desire to be one of the 'submerged ones' – those starving writers in rags who use their manuscripts as a pillow. No! I would put my gift of literary invention to practical use.

AUGUSTUS *wraps a scarf around himself and knocks on another door.*

(*With exaggerated accent, nobility and gravitas.*)
Salutations! My name is Prince Omohoba, possessor of the great gold fields of West Central Africa… I'm looking for lodgings. Just one night will suffice. Payment in advance as is the custom in my country –

LANDLADY (*licking her lips with avarice*). Oooh, your diligence – that will not be necessary certainly – we can h'accommodate you. Sheila – out of the spare room! Your lordship won't mind sharing? That's ten – no, twenty shillings for your first month, and one pound deposit, special price for your lordship.

AUGUSTUS (*aside*). These people will do anything for a quick buck! Let me get this down, for the manuscript!

But by the time I had reached the top of the stairs… I found I was not the only African prince in town.

(*To the occupant of the room.*) John?

John?

JOHN (*resistant*). Augustus. What a coincidence.

'One in a Million' by Aaliyah plays. It continues throughout the rest of the scene.

DUMEBI (*with reference to Aaliyah*). Sorry – but it's such a banger. I said I'd add bits…

He resumes his composure as AUGUSTUS.

I lost no time. I gave him the grand tour…

(*Presentational, to* JOHN.) You will find, my dear Africanus – may I call you Africanus – that London is not what you were taught to expect – it is a land of heathenish barbarians!

See St Paul's Cathedral – House of Prayer! Now in Africa, we worship in church. But Britons do their praying in their bedroom, by night.

(*He does an impression of a couple having sex.*) 'Oh God, oh God, oh Goooooood!'

(*To the audience.*) John's laughing uncontrollably! I press my advantage!

(*To* JOHN *again.*) Behold Africanus! The Bank of England! Enough money in here to buy Sierra Leone one-hundred times over, yet just look around you – have you seen so many beggars in your life, not a trouser leg between them!

Nelson's Column! Cleopatra's Needle! The Houses of Parliament! Big Ben!

The sound of the chime… He stoops, wheezes –

Then there's weather – you expected a mild climate – ha! Truly, it's more like the Ten Plagues of Egypt – you can hardly see your hand in front of you for all this suffocating white fog – !

The music stops. AUGUSTUS *collapses.*

JOHN. 'Sulphur dioxide.'

AUGUSTUS. What?

JOHN. It's not fog. It's 'sulphur dioxide' – poisonous to the lungs. Best to stay off the streets during the day.

AUGUSTUS. As he looks after me, he tells me about his first few months in the metropolis. Of his medical studies. He tells me of his girlfriend in Freetown, Zipporah Cole. She writes him long passionate letters, and he occasionally replies with promises and lies.

DUMEBI (*aside*). Yo. I don't want to stop the flow so lemme just say there's another big parallel. But we don't have time. Lol.

AUGUSTUS. As I recover, I begin to watch him. The way he moves is so familiar.

There's one single bed. We stare at it.

(*To* JOHN, *with insouciance*.) I suppose it's the only way to keep warm in this climate!

JOHN *is drinking something*.

(*To* JOHN.) What's that?

JOHN *pauses. And gives it to* AUGUSTUS.

JOHN. Laudanum – morphine and ethanol. It takes the edge off.

AUGUSTUS *drinks it*.

AUGUSTUS. That night we entangle ourselves in the dark until we forget which limb belongs to whom.

The lights dim, AUGUSTUS *cradles* JOHN *in his arms*.

Love is the best painkiller there is.

Scene Six – Year Two

A cry of 'Happy New Year!' goes up. AUGUSTUS *pulls a party popper, drinks from a bottle of Champagne, and waves a mini Union flag. All of this movement is coordinated to the strains of the National Anthem. This is the New Year's routine.*

AUGUSTUS. My second year with the White Man finds me… poor. I have a notebook full of absurd anecdotes, but no story to hang them on. What struck me as lunatic and absurd in my first year, has begun to sour. What's the point? Who needs to hear it? After a year of grovelling for work it is clear that no African can ever find employment in London. Unless you're performing in a human zoo. Yes you heard me right.

AUGUSTUS *arrives at the 'African Exhibition'…*

ANNOUNCER. Roll up, roll up, for the Pygmies of Central Africa!

AUGUSTUS....As I emerge for air, suddenly one of the Mbuti warriors appears from behind the backdrop, smoking a pack of Taddy's Clown cigarettes.

(*To a Mbuti warrior.*) Jason?! From Freetown...

JASON. Augustus!

What? Law school isn't cheap.

AUGUSTUS *reaches reflexively for his pocket book, opens it – but cannot write. He takes a deep breath.*

AUGUSTUS. There must be another way – and I would find it.

(*To himself.*) Inexhaustible power surges within me... Inexhaustible power surges...

AUGUSTUS *struggles as if through a thick cloying substance that he cannot evade.*

I stumble blindly through the fog to the British Library.

A set of steps illuminate themselves before me.

A path, a prophecy.

AUGUSTUS *sits down and begins to study late into the night.* JOHN *stands near him.*

John listens to me pontificate and strategise. Day after day and night after night he accompanies me here – until the light-bulb moment strikes...

A lamp turns on – without AUGUSTUS *touching it.*

At three a.m. in the reading room.

Within a week of study, I had learned one thing. In this modern Babylon, to succeed, one must build from the bottom.

Scene Seven – Year Three

AUGUSTUS *performs the New Year's routine.*

AUGUSTUS. Year three! I rise.

> AUGUSTUS *is cradling a collection of books. We hear a brisk wind.*

> Speakers' Corner. Where fortune favours the bold.

> AUGUSTUS *clears his throat… no response. He slams the books down on the floor: makes a soap box out of them, which he stands on.*

The whole racket of Empire is based on three simple steps: extract raw materials, manufacture them with cheap labour, then package and sell the goods back to those you stole them off.

(*Aside.*) That got some attention.

My proposition is simple. I will form my own agency, small, mobile, nimble – partnering African business with European distributors. No British brokers or middlemen slurping up the profit.

What say you, friends?

(*Aside.*) I get more than one hundred requests.

Credibility established, I take a trip to all my father's business associates in the kingdom!

Finally, I would have the time and space to write.

(*Clearing throat – to a department-store manager.*) 'I will bring you the finest goods straight to your door, no middleman…'

It works.

He adds more books to the pile and begins to climb.

Yes, the trade protection societies tried to bring me down –

But I outsmarted them.

He wobbles.

Yes John tried to dissuade me.

But I won him over.

He climbs further. He is approaching his dream.

I persuaded regional suppliers to join me from St Albans to Edinburgh.

FACTORY OWNER. I'm sorry, but how can I be sure that an African will pay his bills, sir?

AUGUSTUS. You will be paid in advance – as is the custom in my country.

AUGUSTUS *climbs further.*

I would show my father – that I could be barrister and businessman! And perhaps even something more.

Triumphant now – he reaches the highest point on the staircase of books.

The African General Agency's founder A. B. C. Merriman-Labor declares:

When we convert our cotton to cloth, our rubber to tyres – without letting the foreigner enrich himself by taking these products away – Africa will earn her millions!

AUGUSTUS *imagines the applause. He basks in it.*

But I had miscalculated one thing. I receive a letter from my father.

AUGUSTUS *loses his footing as he reads the letter.*

FATHER (*a formal letter*). 'Sir, you will remove my name from any and all documentation concerning "The General African Agency". I was not consulted, nor have I allowed my name to be used in connection with it. Yours sincerely. Joshua Labor.'

AUGUSTUS. The notice was published in all the major papers. I lost all my clients. He humiliated me.

This lands. An enormous betrayal. The structure collapses.

A beat – he reads his reply.

'Sir, I was at first convinced that you were reluctant to see me succeed as a writer, because you feared for my safety. When you insisted that I pursue law, I consented because I believed you to be trying to ensure my good reputation, knowing all too well what a ruined one looked like. When you demanded that I work for you, I was convinced you did so in order to protect me from the financial hardships that plague so many students in my position. The effort and meagre recompense nearly drove me into the ground. When I secured my own future; when I repaid the kindness you showed to me by struggling for better terms for all African providers, I thought, for one foolish moment, that you might be proud. But your refusal disabused me of my illusions. Your reply displayed a contempt of which I had not thought you capable. You have proved, beyond a shadow of a doubt, that all along your motivation was only spite. It is clear, sir, you cannot abide the thought that your son might succeed where you failed. Since I clearly no longer enjoy your support – filial or financial – henceforth, I suggest you think of me as your loving son, *Augustus Boyle Chamberlayne Merriman, which is how I shall now be known publicly and privately – for I grow tired of Labor.*'

He stares at the note – full of fury. Then patiently, and with calm purpose, shreds it.

The walls of Jericho had come tumbling down in an instant. But I would rebuild them. If I could not use my father's contacts, I would create my own.

AUGUSTUS *rebuilds the pile of books to form a railway carriage. He throws the shredded note out of the carriage window.*

Scene Eight – Year Four

AUGUSTUS *does the New Year's routine.*

AUGUSTUS. My fourth year with the White Man finds me – on a train. The sleeper service from Scotland to London to be precise. John has joined me on my client-finding mission for moral support.

We have the carriage to ourselves.

JOHN. We can't stay here. It's intolerable.

AUGUSTUS. Speak for yourself.

JOHN. So you're happy?

AUGUSTUS. I'm writing…

JOHN. Are you?

AUGUSTUS. I've published articles.

JOHN. Journalists publish articles. Writers publish books.

AUGUSTUS. We all have to start somewhere…

JOHN. And where do these articles appear, Augustus? *The Times*? *The Telegraph*? The *Daily Mail*?

AUGUSTUS. You know very well where they appear – *The Sierra Leone Weekly Times* – what of it?

JOHN. Who will read this book of yours when you have finished? Who will care? What are you writing? Scraps you lock up in your desk drawer for fear someone might read them. What if they actually find out what you really think of this place? You'll be hounded out of the country!

(JOHN *imitates him.*) The White Man will come to get you Augustus! The White Man will come and take you away…!

We should be with our people.

AUGUSTUS. I am… a British subject. As are you.

JOHN. Oh really! You see yourself anywhere here? Look around you. Shameful…

AUGUSTUS. Shameful. Why did you say shameful?

JOHN. You know why I say that. Your… our way of life here is…

AUGUSTUS. It's what?

JOHN. Irreligious.

AUGUSTUS. Irreligious? What is a more religious precept
than fraternity? Jesus and John had a fairly intimate and
well-documented relationship, didn't they?

JOHN. Oh I'm beginning to see your problem, Augustus. You
think you're the Messiah.

AUGUSTUS (*aside*). A stony silence. It stretches for minutes.

JOHN. Augustus… Zipporah and I – we're engaged.

AUGUSTUS (*aside*). Betrayal is a funny thing. It can wake you
up, or put you to sleep. And it woke me UP!

We arrive in London that evening – waiting for us on the
platform is…

ZIPPORAH. Zipporah, Zipporah Cole.

AUGUSTUS. Charmed, charmed.

ZIPPORAH. I've heard so much about you! You're all anyone
is talking about in Freetown.

She brandishes a newspaper.

AUGUSTUS. Life must have gotten far less stimulating since
I left.

ZIPPORAH. John never stops talking about you –

AUGUSTUS. He's prone to hyperbole. The effects of an
imperial climate no doubt.

ZIPPORAH. It's not just him who thinks so.

(*She reads*.) 'Organising the beautiful ceremony in
commemorating the centenary of the abolition of the slave
trade at Westminster Abbey is Merriman-Labor, a gentle,
pleasant and highly educated Negro… who says he is proud
to be called a Black Englishman.'

AUGUSTUS. I wouldn't believe everything you read in the
press.

ZIPPORAH. With all this publicity, surely a book is on the cards?

Oh, where are my manners, Augustus, this is my father –

JC COLE *rises and offers his hand.*

JC COLE. JC Cole... quite the fan.

ZIPPORAH. You will dine with us this evening?

AUGUSTUS. I'm afraid – I regret –

JC COLE. When you are next in Africa, call on me... I could help raise funds for you to publish.

ZIPPORAH. You won't deny us your company on our last night.

AUGUSTUS. Your last night?

ZIPPORAH. We will be staying with Father for a few weeks – John is to meet the family. I'm afraid it will be unutterably dull for him. Do let's celebrate together?

JC COLE. Don't worry – I won't be joining. It'll just be the three of you.

AUGUSTUS. He leans in close.

JC COLE. Zipporah has a sister... yes? Think about it, my son.

AUGUSTUS. I take them to the music hall. We laugh. Drink. Parade the streets. An odd trio. But all through it, I have this awful certainty, it will be my last memory of John. Zipporah matches us drink for drink... at first.

ZIPPORAH. John, take me home.

AUGUSTUS. He's back half an hour later. We terrorise the streets for hours. I don't want it to end. When we are thrown out of the last club, I am so drunk, I break into a run every time I see a police officer. They chase after me like lapdogs until I turn and face them, monocle and bow tie in full view.

POLICE OFFICER. Why are you running?

AUGUSTUS. Can't a man run? Of a sumptuous evening such as this?

POLICE OFFICER. Move on...

AUGUSTUS. Certainly, officer. We cackle and lurch our way home.

We rolled into the house so drunk, we didn't wait to turn the lights on in the corridor.

Zipporah is spark out on the drawing-room chair. Before we can think better of it, John and I find ourselves in my room, as if by habit.

It hadn't occurred to me to change the sheets...

JOHN *kisses him passionately.*

We fall at one another so violently we don't hear the stirrings below, Zipporah on the stairs, nor when the door opens.

Long beat.

He chased after her, half-naked down the street.

I waited until dawn for his return, before succumbing to sleep. When I awoke, mere hours later, it was to an empty house. He had taken everything. His clothes, medical equipment, papers, books.

Morning came with a knock at the door. Mail for Mr Merriman-Labor! Though my head was pounding and my eyes were bleary, I recognised the typeface. A summons from Lincoln's Inn.

The sound of a gavel transports us to the courthouse.

JUDGE 1. It has come to our attention, Mr Labor – that you have authorised the use of your name in connection with this legal society for the purposes of business. Is this true?

AUGUSTUS. It is true that I manage the African General Agency, yes.

JUDGE 2. A business venture of a somewhat objectionable nature if your advertisements are anything to go by. Who is the author of this circular?

He pushes a sheet of paper towards him.

AUGUSTUS. I am, sir.

JUDGE 1. Indeed? You claim to offer consultation on: African Affairs, Agriculture, Amusements, Arts and Astrology, Banks, Commerce, Education, Freemasonry, Medicine, Mining, Palmistry, Patents...

JUDGE 2 (*wryly amused*). Is that all?

JUDGE 1. It is clear from a cursory glance that your 'enterprise' is wholly inconsistent with the character of this Society. We will be compelled to strike your name – unless… you give an unconditional undertaking to terminate all commercial ventures under this name.

He bashes a ceremonial gavel.

Oh – before you go. It may interest you to note, you have passed the bar examinations with honours. Your essay was awarded a distinction, 'Define an Act of God'. Commendable. Most commendable. Nevertheless, you shall not be formally admitted into this Society until we are in receipt of your notice of termination of the African General Agency – and all other such 'ventures'. There is time yet to redeem yourself, young man. Such is the lassitude of British justice. Good day, Mr Labor.

AUGUSTUS. I stand on the centre of Tower Bridge, watching the seething waves beneath.

Scene Nine – Soho House

DUMEBI. Having fun? Yeah.

He gets a small towel to wipe away the sweat.

I didn't see Alfred for fifteen years, and the first time I saw him after that gap I was waiting on him. So I used to do front of house at this members' club, and sometimes when we were understaffed I'd help out with serving members. Alfred was speaking at one of the events they held for Black History Month; he and David Olusoga were discussing the enduring relationship between modern Britain and people whose origins lie in Africa.

DUMEBI *laughs.*

Sorry, I'm not laughing at that, it's just hilarious, I worked there for two, three years and you gotta love these vapid elitist companies that so blatantly put on events and get all these speakers with their blue ticks to just 'speak on' shit, whatever that means.

'Amplifying voices.'

No, sorry, I'm being cynical, it's just – yeah, it's interesting…

If Alfred was here he would remind me of the significance of said events – the necessity of them. He always used to say:

ALFRED (*recorded*). On these shoulders we ride.

DUMEBI. On these shoulders we ride.

> DUMEBI *laughs. The memory of Alfred's voice is overwhelming. He's transported for a moment into the past. It's as if he's right there in front of him.*

Whatever the fuck that means.

But anyway, Alfred's doing a talk, and I see his name on the programme when I start my shift and I'm like… mad. Alfred Sesay, ya know. There was this black-and-white photo of him sitting in a library with this old huge book in front of him, that he clearly wasn't reading, and he had these glasses… those glasses… gosh those glasses were horrible. He was cute though, I can remember thinking he looked cute.

No, he was cute, I'll give him that. Oh, you guys do know it's him on the poster? Yeah, yeah – he had it all prepped. My Uncle Frank, he's not actually my uncle, it's just a cultural thing for those who don't know. But, yeah he owns a shop, Lipman and Sons, and they sell dinner suits, tailcoats and frock coats. He let Alfred have the stuff for free if a) he could have the photos for the website and b) if he plugged the shop, so, yeah Twenty-Two Charing Cross Road, if you fancy, you can hire and buy.

Right.

After the discussion, he still hadn't noticed me, so I just went up to him.

DUMEBI. Alfred Sesay!!

ALFRED. Er… Oh, gosh. Dumebi!!

DUMEBI. Haha, how are you, man?

ALFRED. Yeah, I'm good, I'm good – so good to see you!

DUMEBI (*internal*). Silence… nah, is this awkward? Surely, it's not awkward. How are you?

ALFRED. Yeah, I'm good man, how's – how's – how's your family?

DUMEBI. All good, everyone is good – saw you up there, well done, you spoke so well.

ALFRED. Haha, no, thank you. I was a bit unprepared for those questions.

DUMEBI. No, you weren't, you did great – do you want another drink?

ALFRED. Yeah, sure – what brings you to the talk?

DUMEBI. Oh, I work here. Drinks on me – [Wink wink.]

ALFRED. Haha! Aren't the drinks free anyway?

DUMEBI. Haha, yet it was a joke.

ALFRED. Oh, haha!

DUMEBI *stares at* ALFRED *and* ALFRED *stares back.*

DUMEBI (*to the audience*). Okay, okay so it was a bit awkward but like good awkward, there was a vibe – and it was potent.

Anyway, so he knows where I work now. I swear before that day I'd never seen him since...

Then guess who starts popping up all the time. At least once a week from then on, I'd see him.

ALFRED. Just going for a swim, and I'd thought I'd say hi.

Just meeting a friend for coffee, and I thought I'd say hi.

Just going for the screening, and I'd thought I'd say hi.

DUMEBI. FYI Alfred can't swim and he hates coffee – he's just got it bad.

Our initial chats were awkward.

DUMEBI *stares at* ALFRED *again and again* ALFRED *stares back.*

But it'd ease up and we just chatted about anything and everything, mainly music.

ANTI, Rihanna's last studio album – mad – had come out a few months back and the way me and this man unpacked that body of work.

We had this massive argument over Drake's line in 'Work' – 'If you had a twin, I would still choose you'. Alfred thought it was quote 'iconic'. I could not relate. I'd hope that if you were my partner, you'd still 'choose me' if I had a twin, and that that kinda would go unsaid, Drake – I don't know.

We actually disagreed a lot. Old Alfred and I, not in a negative way though.

DUMEBI *laughs*.

One of the days he shows up and asks if I want to go see Rihanna on tour. *Issa* date, he's not calling it a date but we all know *issa* date. I immediately agreed, even though all the tickets had sold out in Wembley and the tickets he got were for Old Trafford, in Manchester.

He asked me before he told me.

We'd 'have to stay' overnight because we'd miss the last train back, that's what he said, but I'm pretty sure there would have been one we could have caught.

I went, we stayed at a Holiday Inn, and boy did we find love in a hopeless place.

Perhaps the intro for 'Work' plays on loop.

I think that was one of the best nights of my life – Ri killed it, naturally, and yeah it was just so, so special – he'd…

Nah actually, wait, so I spoke to my therapist and told her I was doing this and she said I should remember to keep some things for myself, for us, and so we'll leave that night at that – it was really special, yeah, really.

Pause. A moment.

I'm going to refrain from saying something like '*that was the first of many special nights*' but that's kinda where the story goes – I couldn't tell you all of them because, yeah there were so many in our years together.

We had sex in a fridge once.

DUMEBI *is silently laughing to himself*.

But that's not relevant.

(*To tech box*.) How long do we have?

The TECHNICIAN *replies.*

Fuck, yeah anyway – we fell in love.

Cue montage, except I don't have one – just imagine, suspend your belief – that's what it says in *The Art of Dramatic Writing.*

Gosh – (*He says how much time is left.*)

Actually no.

I will tell you about Uju's wedding. So for the first one maybe two years we dated, both our families did that typical Nigerian – I know Alfred isn't Nigerian but we are Africa, so, sorry, we just are. Anyway, they did that typical '*they are just really good friends*' when it came to Alfred and I. We were the BEST of friends, so close – me and my friend. In the summer of 2018 my sister got married. His name was, wow, his name *is* Jonathan, and he works in recruitment, I'm not judging. Alfred and I went together, like together together, hand in hand and it was a lot – my first act of defiance, that's what Alfred was like, defiant, he was pretty fearless.

Scene Nine – Year Five

AUGUSTUS *pulls a party popper.*

AUGUSTUS. And so it has come to this.

To be a writer, I must be published. But no reputation, no publication.

To gain a reputation, I must become a barrister. But to be a barrister, I must be a gentleman.

Gentlemen do not work. To be a writer, I must throw away my life savings and any prospect of income in the future.

I must humiliate the family, I intend to support – to be a writer I must become a beggar.

And, begging is illegal in the imperial capital.

But, how could I show my face back home?

At that moment, a beggar approaches the island.

His appearance is pitiable.

He coughs.

BEGGAR. Spare some change, kind sir…

AUGUSTUS. I dig around in my pockets and raise sixpence. He shuffles off thanking me.

No sooner is he ten yards away, he screams racist abuse and runs as fast as his shuffling limbs will carry him.

I mean, what the fuck is the point?!

At that moment, I saw a bus careering around our small island in the centre of the road.

A one-word advert is emblazoned in enormous letters across its broadside: 'TRAVELOGUE' – beside it: the beaming bespectacled face of a lecturer.

A sign from the universe: a third way, where business and writing meets – a new destiny: the travelling lecturer!

Soundscape of the sea – once again. Foghorn!

I am out on the open sea, the SS *Karina* powering towards the Tropics. I have the wind in my face, my lecture notes under my arm, a projector in my trunk and spite on my tongue.

My field notes from my stay in this barbarous land have taken shape. The title is obvious.

Five Years with the White Man – a survival guide for the intrepid traveller.

I arrive in Freetown bay amidst some of the worst rains I had seen in my life. My sodden family battle to stay upright.

FATHER. Son… I've missed you.

AUGUSTUS (*to* FATHER). And I you.

Beside him is John's mother, Mary.

MARY. Augustus!

How is John? He didn't come with you?

AUGUSTUS *has avoided the question. The lights snap and suddenly,* AUGUSTUS *is delivering a lecture.*

AUGUSTUS. Ladies and gentlemen, I give you – London!

He projects an image of the imperial capital!

Land of ignorance, land of poverty, land… of the White Man.

He projects an image of London.

See how multitudes upon multitudes rush hither and thither, helter-skelter-like, with so much motion and commotion, verging and converging in all directions –

The lights snap once again. We return to the suppressed conversation at the dockside. It has the quality of an intrusive thought.

FATHER. I didn't warn you against writing because I thought you'd fail, I feared you would succeed – and you would kill yourself in the process.

AUGUSTUS (*comically searching for visible cracks in his body*). I'm still in one piece, aren't I?

MARY. Augustus, your father's right, you cannot stay in London indefinitely.

AUGUSTUS. And why not?

FATHER. There comes a time in life, where one must face reality!

Snap back to the lecture.

AUGUSTUS. Even in your own home, I know, colour puts impediment in your way. And do not reckon on charity in London. Remember we have already been weaned from the suckling period of sympathy and philanthropy. We have now to creep, stand, or walk for ourselves without the help of a nurse's hand!

Now, cuisine. They say, the French eat frogs. But so does the Briton. Toad in the hole!

Snap back to the dock.

FATHER. Augustus, who do you think you are helping? Where are your audience? Here? There? Or just inside the confines of your thick skull? Remember your first book, you were still a boy when I had it published for you, remember the title you gave it: *Building Castles in the Air*! That's become your life's work – hasn't it? Rest assured, Augustus, your exercise in fantasy edifies no one.

AUGUSTUS. It's not fantasy.

FATHER. Then what is it?

AUGUSTUS. Faith.

FATHER. Faith? Faith in what?

Beat. Snap back to the lecture.

AUGUSTUS. But the true spirit of Britain lies not in its great cathedrals, nor its parliament, but in the theatre and music hall. For there one sees the pick and prime of England's youth and beauty… Do not ask me to comment on the respective merits of English girls and those from Sierra Leone, nor which I prefer. I cannot answer your question, because I have never loved, nor have I ever been loved.

Snap back to the dock.

MARY. When you see John, you'll tell him to write, won't you? We miss him.

FATHER. What should I tell the family?

Snap back to the lecture.

AUGUSTUS *projects an image of the Royal Family and the strains of the anthem resound.*

AUGUSTUS. Please, all be upstanding now for the National Anthem.

Stand up. STAND UP!

The anthem swells and then fades.

Hello the Gambia! Liberia! Senegal!

Finally, I reach Zungeru – and there stands the woman who left me all those years ago. My mother. But next to her is the Deputy Governor. He bars me from performing.

DEPUTY GOVERNOR. We have promised to stop the local people adopting too many European customs. We find they have a bad effect. Your lecture has been deemed… well, you understand I'm sure.

AUGUSTUS. Too well.

> *In a flash we see* AUGUSTUS *become the White Bogey Man. He laughs after terrorising the audience.* AUGUSTUS *carefully places the mask down. He addresses it – like Hamlet does the skull of Yorick.*

> In England, I am told I should be with my people. Yet when I am in Africa, you authorities find reasons to keep us apart. Now why is that?

GILLIAN. Augustus, there is only one reason I have found for all the sadness in the world. It's there to show us how much we love.

> Have faith, my son. Inexhaustible power surges within you.

> AUGUSTUS *laughs.*

Scene Ten – Return

AUGUSTUS *walks through the New Year sequence once again – it has become very mechanical. He is rushing to return 'home'.*

AUGUSTUS. I formally terminate the AGA. Pay off all creditors. There is nothing left to do, but to write up the manuscript – mine the notebooks, articles, lectures. It takes a few weeks, all my memories surging together, in one bundle.

> I let my father's letters pile up. I know what they contain: entreaties to return, to be with my people.

> I finish the book, deep in debt – and happy.

> At the last minute I change the title from *Five Years with the White Man* to *Britons Through Negro Spectacles* in the hope of finding a publisher. The manuscript is posted so many times, its corners grow dog-eared.

> Rejection.

> Rejection.

> Rejection.

DUMEBI. What's new?

AUGUSTUS. I tap JC Cole for investment, my father's associates, old acquaintances – and self-publish in grand style.

The *Express*. I'm reviewed in the *Express*!

(*Reading*.) 'Causes have been won for the Negro in the past, but not in this way. If the Negro is worthy of being put on a level with the White Man, nothing will eventually keep him from that place.'

He throws the paper away –

The reviews in Britain are horrible. The reviews in West Africa are… non-existent.

Sales tank. I'm bankrupt in weeks. I keep reading the papers, for any further mentions. Nothing.

There is nothing left to say. Words dry up.

I'm standing on the centre point of Tower Bridge. A handful of coins in my hands, hardly enough for food. My last.

A steamer is about to pass through. Looking down at the surging Thames below, I consider throwing myself into it as the gates rise. Ending my days between the two panels of one bridge. Between two worlds.

At that moment, a shuffling man approaches me.

I'm about to tell him I have no change, when I see his face. Cadaverous. Familiar. John?

Tears come to his eyes the moment he sees me.

JOHN. It wasn't going to work, was it.

AUGUSTUS. Zipporah?

JOHN *shakes his head.*

I thought you would have been home by now?

JOHN. As soon as I'm better.

JOHN *coughs.*

Tuberculosis. I'm told.

AUGUSTUS. He's lost so much weight. I have to carry him through the streets to my lodgings. He stops for breath every thirty yards.

By next week, he can't walk.

I fill his room with flowers from Covent Garden –

Book a singer from the music halls to sing to him through the window.

'Girls, Girls' – a music-hall song – echoes.

JOHN. Augustus, do you think one day someone will make sense of everything?

AUGUSTUS. Of everything?

JOHN. Of this.

AUGUSTUS. I shouldn't think so. By the time they could understand it, no one would remember.

JOHN. I expect you're right.

AUGUSTUS *mutters a silent prayer beside his bed.*

AUGUSTUS. In his last days, John is shaking with febrile energy. Hungry for details of my trip.

JOHN. My mother, she was smiling?

AUGUSTUS (*to* JOHN). She can't wait to see you –

A long beat. AUGUSTUS *caresses* JOHN's *hair.*

But his breathing is laboured now. Every word costs effort.

JOHN. Publish. Don't go home. Not until it's done. Publish.

AUGUSTUS. I promise. I stroke his hair.

JOHN. Thank you for finding me.

AUGUSTUS. I stay with him long after he passes. I want time with him before they take him.

The day his body is removed for burial, I receive a certificate in the post.

He receives the paper.

I have passed the bar. I am a legalised and licensed lawyer. My father sends congratulations.

He looks at the papers for a long time. Was it worth it?

He slowly shreds them with increasing resolution.

I head to the music hall.

On impulse, I book two seats.

Scene Eleven – Epilogue

DUMEBI. So yeah. A. B. C. was a forgotten footnote in history. On his shoulders we ride.

Until now. Penguin is republishing his shit. Bernardine Evaristo editing. Oooh, if Alfred could see this.

Alfred left some notes about A. B. C.'s final months, but died before he could finish them… so I've just summarised.

(*Reading.*) A. B. C. got into a dispute over a suit. Lincoln's Inn disbarred him for 'bringing the society into disrepute'. I'm not going to say it broke him, but let's just say, he stopped believing in British justice. He survived the First World War, survived the Spanish flu pandemic that killed his dad and his sisters and Zipporah. He never stopped writing. He changed his name, to Ohlohr Maigi, which is the name on his death certificate. Was on the verge of recognition. Then, at that moment, he caught TB – and passed.

I said we're not doing the death. And we're not. He died in Lambeth Infirmary. His landlady paid for his funeral.

At his memorial in Sierra Leone, his uncle said that he was a man who 'dabbled his head in journalism and literature… but could not be prevailed on to be with his people'.

The end. Ha. Yeah, I'm as confused as you to be honest.

It wasn't all true by the way. Not all of it. John's fiancée's invented.

Oh and we can't truly say John and A. B. C. were lovers. I mean, the bruddah never married, they clearly loved their night-life together oh and I did a Zoom with his biographer as she said:

(*Reading*.) 'I wouldn't be surprised.'

…but sure, we 'don't know'. Look if you want to know the truth, read the book.

Oh, shit shit shit. Which reminds me.

One last thing.

The ending he planned was meant to be – the very last bit from A. B. C.'s book. He couldn't adapt it.

So I'll just play this…

ALFRED *is unwell, he sounds tired – but his work clearly gives him energy.*

ALFRED (*voicemail*). Notes for final scene…

Right. Don't know exactly how this is going to work but… maybe just have A. B. C. step out of character, like what happens at the end of… *BlacKkKlansman*, where they do the jump-cut to the Trump rallies… and have the actor just tell the story of when I tracked down A. B. C.'s great-nephew and he told this mad story about coming to London for the first time in the eighties, and the person he was meant to meet at Victoria Station hadn't turned up, and he is bewildered and alone in the middle of London and then someone from Sierra Leone comes up to him – what are the chances – and accompanies him all the way to his uncle's address – and just before he waves him goodbye, he asks him his name and he says Johnny – and how I had to end the call, because I was crying and I blamed it on the Wi-Fi being fucked up.

ALFRED *begins to cough. We hear a voice from the other room.*

DUMEBI (*voice-over*). You okay?

ALFRED (*voice-over*). Yep. Good.

A beat. DUMEBI *is visibly moved. The recording continues.*

…remember to clean the fridge.

The recording ends.

DUMEBI. Excuse the coughing. He wasn't well.

He wasn't well.

You know, I spoke to his friend, Vanessa, who works in
theatre. Well, she teaches GCSE drama, but we move. Yeah,
so when Vanessa told me the play wasn't long enough and
I said I'm gonna just fill in the bits with things about Alfred
and I, she was like: they'll wanna know how he died. I said it
wasn't anyone's fucking business. But then in *The Art of
Dramatic Writing* it says 'death is a climax'. So, I thought...
fuck it, here we go, I'll give you the climax.

Laughs. He finds this difficult.

Alfred died of stage-four prostate... cancer – we tried
hormone therapy but...

Yeah.

I've been thinking a lot about why I did this – and what the
universe was trying to tell me with this whole thing that I'm
doing.

I think I've worked it out. Yeah.

He takes out a piece of paper and reads the next bit.

'This is a recognition and act of thanksgiving for the
indomitable spirit that courses through people who imagine
a truth that doesn't yet exist, and through sheer force of love –
make it come about in the world. One for the bellowers.' Ha.

I love you, Alfred. On *your* shoulders *I* ride.

Laughs.

Ha. That sounds sexual.

Climax.

Sorry.

*He folds the piece of paper back up, takes a moment and
says...*

Thanks for being involved in my personal act of
bereavement therapy.

It's done.

You can go home now. Peace.

Aaliyah's 'One in a Million' plays him off.

HONOUR-BOUND

Zahra Jassi

*For young Brown actors
fed up with one-dimensional roles*

ZAHRA JASSI

Zahra Jassi is an actor, writer, and theatre-maker from the East Midlands and based in London. She is a recent graduate of King's College London, and is a student at Identity School of Acting. She is also a member of the Almeida Theatre's Youth Advisory Board and has a particular interest in EDI within the arts sector. She enjoys exploring themes of race, injustice, culture, power and intersectionality, and empowering artists of colour through her writing and theatre-making. Zahra is passionate about the substantive representation of artists of colour in the dramatic arts and can't wait to write more plays and create opportunities for them. *Honour-Bound* marks Zahra's professional writing and acting debut.

Honour-Bound was first performed at VAULT Festival, London, on 7 March 2023, with the following cast:

SIMRAN   Zahra Jassi
MUSICIAN   Ahana Hundal

Dramaturg   Karla Crome
Lighting and Sound   Steven J. Poland
Illustrator   Mariam Abdurahman

122

Acknowledgements

Nick Hern Books for the opportunity. Bec Martin and the amazing people at VAULT Festival for the opportunity.

Karla Crome for her guidance. Steven J. Poland for stepping in at the eleventh hour and buying me emotional-support pints of cider. Ahana Hundal (you just have to listen to understand why). Mariam Abdurahman for her patience and vision.

Professor Aisha K. Gill for her expertise.

The staff at The Eaglet for facilitating the emotional-support pints of cider.

My family and friends. Lola.

Z.J.

'It should be called the Devil's work. Honour has nothing to do with it at all. It's dishonour. Disloyalty'

Bekhal Mahmod

Characters

SIMRAN, *twenty years old. British-Indian woman. English*
accent
MUSICIAN

A DLR-train carriage. Daytime.

SIMRAN, *wearing Jordans and a comfortable airport outfit, is stood next to a chair, looking around at audience members. She stays on some longer than others.*

She examines their eyes, their clothing, what they're doing.

She thinks of reasons they're on the train, what's going on in their lives.

She acknowledges their consciousness.

Next to the chair is a suitcase. Inside the suitcase are clothes, a loofah, and other props detailed throughout the script. A VK Blue bottle and a bottle opener are downstage-right on the floor. A plate with four slices of bread, some sandwich meat and some lettuce, a knife, a plate with two pakore on, a mug, and a slice of toast with a bite taken out of it are on a small table on the other side of the chair. A handful of red petals and two small candles are downstage-centre on the floor. There's a bin downstage-left.

(*Fades back to reality.*) I always end up doing this when I'm travelling. And it's weird because I did a module on this last term, and it was so strange reading about something that you experience but you didn't know it had a name or was even a thing like that. So, it's called sonder. It's basically where you realise that other people have lives that you don't know anything about. So, whenever I'm on the train I'll have my headphones in, and I always end up losing myself. And like ten minutes later I'll kind of click back into reality and realise that for the past ten minutes I've been staring at someone and thinking up scenarios of why they're on the train: where they're going and why, where they live, what job they have, who their friends and family are, what problems they have.

Beat.

Right now, I don't think any of their problems will be quite as big as mine which is annoying because I usually rely on thinking that they will be to make mine seem small. And I always feel so bad because I've been staring at them for ages and that's just awkward. But it's also just such a wild thing to think about because I know none of the answers to any of the questions I ask about them. I say, 'I know' and now I've opened a rabbit hole of whether we can ever truly know something, or prove something, what truth is, what reality is... And then you just feel so small and insignificant –

(*Someone offers their seat*.) 'Oh, thank you.' (*Sits*.)

Yeah, you just feel so small and insignificant and alone and... well I usually reach my stop by then to be honest but yeah. Basically, philosophy is scary. And it becomes even scarier because there's this school of thought called solipsism. And according to that school of thought, no one can prove that they're conscious in the same way you are. Like if you ask your mum to prove she's conscious to you – how does she do that? She can't. And so, because people can't prove that they're conscious like you are, no one else is conscious and you're the only conscious being in, like, the whole world or the whole universe.

Sigh.

So, um, yeah... I don't really enjoy taking the train.

But I'm going to meet my boyfriend at the airport who will hopefully make me feel a bit better and a bit safer, so I will just keep myself to myself and firm this train ride.

We've not seen each other in ages. Well, it's been a week or so, but it feels like ages. I've been staying at a friend's place in Islington for about a week and he's been staying at a friend's place in Lambeth and... I really miss him and can't wait to see him. It's been a lot. We text each other twice a day – morning and night – just to let each other know we're okay, and that's it. 'Hi, I'm awake.' 'Hi, so am I.' 'Goodnight.' 'Goodnight.' Raunchy, I know. We don't wanna send 'incriminating' texts. I know it probably sounds crazy, but I just don't want my family to somehow hack my phone or iCloud or something and find the texts – even though we've sent way worse.

His name's Jay. We met about two years ago when I was in first year. We're on the same course – he's a year above me, but yeah, same course – philosophy. We met at Philosophy Society –

PhilSoc. Yeah, we really bonded and clicked over the Logical
Problem of Evil and The Trolley Problem – super-romantic,
fairy-tale stuff, you know – classic PhilSoc. No, I actually didn't
get along with him at first. He debated so agressively and he was
so loud and –

(*To someone on the train.*) 'I'm sorry I don't have any change.'

Beat.

I do have change and I feel awful lying about it. I'm only using
cash at the moment, but I haven't worked for a week so can't
really afford to give any away.

Beat.

The few times I saw Jay after that PhilSoc social were also in
group settings and we didn't really talk that much. Then there was
a big PhilSoc night out at Ministry, you know, Ministry Tuesdays,
and everyone went. And that was when things started to change.
I'd decided I wasn't gonna go earlier in the day. The Tottenham
game started late that evening, so I didn't think I'd be able to get
ready and make it there in time for last entry, and I really wanted
to watch that game, so I had decided not to go. But my friend
Atticus – yes, Atticus, what a name for a philosopher – he was
texting me saying 'Please come out – it'll be a great night', blah
blah blah and I get bad FOMO so I'm like 'Okay, fine, fine, I'll
go.' The game's not finished though so I bring my straighteners
into the living room and start doing my hair in the ninety-seventh
minute. I'm on a time crunch, last entry is at twelve, and it's ten-
thirty because the game went to extra time. Son had scored but it
was ruled offside. Fucking VAR. It's ruining the beautiful English
game. I'm straightening my last section of hair when Vardy scores
an absolute screamer. Top bins. Annoying but credit where
credit's due, great goal. And I burnt my neck reacting to it but
there's no time to treat it, so I soldier on.

By half-time my hair is done. One-hundred-and-fifth minute.
I start choosing an outfit. Probably should have done that first
because this really slows me down and I take until the hundred-
and-twelfth minute to decide. I settle on a skirt and a crop top.
People have probably seen this get-up before, but I look good in
it, I couldn't wear this sort of thing at home, and there's just no
time so ye old faithful it is. Clothes are on and then I look down

and realise my legs are prickly. Not hairy but there's just too much hair for me to feel comfortable going out in a skirt and I've already committed to the outfit now, so the only option is a quick shave. I can't wet my legs now there's no time and I don't wanna ruin my outfit with shaving cream… so it's gonna have to be a dry shave.

I grab a razor from my shower and start on my right leg. The pain is immediate and the blood's not far behind. I soldier on. Left leg. Done. Quick rinse – get the hairs off. One-hundred-and-twenty-second minute – I start my make-up. One-hundred-and-twenty-third minute Kane with a tap-in. I'm ecstatic, but mascara goes on my right eyelid during my celebration. But two–one! But there's no time. I'm actually a pro at doing my make-up quickly so by the time I'm done I look really good, and we've won the game. *And* I captained Kane on my fantasy team that week so double points for me!

I check the state of my legs, grab a couple plasters and just slap them on. Also, because I dry-shaved, I've got scratch marks on me. And because I'm brown the scratch marks are white, so they really show up on my skin and are starting to sting tons, but, I mean, it is what it is at this point. Legs aside though, I look good. I run to the kitchen and start making a drink for the Tube journey over. I grab a plastic bottle and pour vodka in it… and then realise I haven't got any mixer. Great. Well, there's oat milk – no no! Then this half-empty orange Lucozade Sport bottle catches my eye, and I don't have anything else – it's that or the oat milk – so I take it and I pour it in. It's been sitting out since yesterday so it's really warm, but then I think 'Would it make a difference if it was cold?' I don't know, it's still vodka and Lucozade Sport isn't it.

I speed-walk to the Tube station and hop on the train. I'm texting Atticus. I type 'omw' and press send but autocorrect always changes that to 'on my way exclamation mark', and it makes you look really keen and not cool like you do when you abbreviate stuff. I'm embarrassed. But then I remember my name isn't Atticus, so I feel better! There's a Pakistani family on the train sat near me laughing and pointing at my legs. Joke's on them though really isn't it. Indian food's way better. I get off at Elephant and Castle and sprint to Ministry. The queue is pretty long, but I'm like 'Well at least I've got my drink, I can just pre in the queue', but then I take a sip of my drink and remember it tastes like ass! Warm ass! The queue moves quickly though. I'm near the front. I hold my nose, down my drink, and chuck the bottle. I gag like once or twice, it's okay. I give the bouncer my ID, he calls me pretty – I feel validated, and he lets me in. (*Exhale.*) We made it. We are in the club.

A hip-hop beat plays.

And the PhilSoc crew has basically taken over the whole of the RnB room, lovely stuff. I grab a drink from the bar – 'double gin and lemonade please'. I wish I liked tonic or soda water because it just sounds cooler saying 'G&T' instead of 'gin and lemonade', but I don't. Tonic water and soda water taste like TV static. There's no other way to describe it and I know it doesn't make sense, but also it does make sense. I find my friends on the dance floor. They're waved and I hate playing catch-up. Amrita's on my left, double-fisting two blue VKs and using them to fist-pump above her head. They spill all over her. She either doesn't notice or doesn't care but she's in a white top so... Atticus is next to her. He doesn't have a drink in his hand, but he's got two finger-guns and white clout goggles on. And next to him is our other friend Sam. She's as basic as white girls come. (*Thinking.*) Yeah, she really doesn't have any quirks I can mention here, but she's great. She's great. I spend the night drinking, dancing, and chatting to PhilSoc people. I'm on the dance floor and Amrita is on her next set of two blue VKs. I genuinely don't know how she likes those. Like she doesn't just drink them and tolerate them, she *likes* them. It's her drink of choice. I don't know how her teeth have any enamel left. And also, I'm sorry but it just has to be said, how is 'blue' a flavour? She's still fist-pumping with them but this time they spill all over my legs and sting like a bitch because, oh yeah, I dry-shaved.

The music's good though. Jay and some of his friends come over. They say hi, we say hi. We merge our groups and dance together. And let me tell you something: the boy can dance. He's so... rhythmic, and so are his friends, it's so cool. I don't wanna seem weird, but I can't take my eyes off him.

The hip-hop beat slowly fades out. MUSICIAN *plays 'Tere Bin Nahin Lagda' by Nusrat Fateh Ali Khan on the acoustic guitar.*

I don't know if it's because I've been drinking or what, but
I feel a little… something inside of me and I'm just seeing him
in a different way. He's smiling and having fun and he doesn't
seem aggressive like he did the first time we met. He looks up
and we catch eyes… and I don't look away. He looks kinda
concerned though. He comes over, leans down to my ear and
asks if I'm okay. I lean into his ear and say 'Yeah, why?' He
looks down and says, 'Well, your legs look really painful.' For
fuck's sake. I reply 'Yeah, but Tottenham won.' And he looks at
me with playful disgust and I realise he's an Arsenal fan. That's
disappointing, but there's still something inside me that's
intrigued by him tonight. The white T-shirt he's wearing really
suits him, the sleeves hug his arms and accentuate his muscles
really nicely. I didn't realise how built he was before. Like he
could win a fight. We all carry on dancing and before I know it
the night's over and I'm scoffing some cheesy chips waiting for
my Uber home –

MUSICIAN *stops playing*.

I get in the Uber and all I can think about is him. Then I go out
on the Friday of that week, and a Black guy catches my eye at
the bar. Normally, I might entertain that, but it was just nothing
compared to how I felt with Jay. So, I look away.

Limehouse Station announcement. SIMRAN *sits*.

So, yeah, after that PhilSoc night out we kind of were okay with
each other. Friendly with each other. I'd say hi to him round
campus, we followed each other on Instagram. And I looked
forward to seeing him. It was weird.

And then in May of first year we got really close. We were both
going through a really horrible time, and we leant on each other.
Basically, Amrita died in May of first year – or she was killed.
She was killed. She was promised to someone. His name was
Aman, he was Indian. I never met him, but he lived in
Whitechapel, so they lived pretty close. He was a family friend
that her parents liked. But Amrita didn't like him. He was nice
enough, but she didn't *like* him. She didn't think he was fit, or
funny, or… I don't know they just didn't click how you're
supposed to with someone you're gonna marry. And she
eventually started talking to this other guy – Rishi – also Indian,

who she *really* liked. The way you are supposed to like
someone like that. Rishi went to uni in West London, so he
lived in Paddington. She would always travel to him to see him,
she felt safer in West London because her family and Aman
were in East.

Pause.

I think what she forgot though was that *my* family moved West.
We moved to Hounslow, but they would go to White City
sometimes... and my brother saw them once. He was with my
mum and one of my mum's friends from Whitechapel and he
saw Amrita and Rishi – just holding hands. And he said to my
mum, 'Oh, look, it's Amrita', and my mum looked and realised
that she wasn't holding hands with Aman. She didn't know who
Rishi was. And she told Amrita's parents what she'd seen and
that it wasn't just my brother Arun and my mum who saw, but
that her friend from Whitechapel was there and saw as well, so
I think they knew that it was just a matter of time before other
people in Shadwell knew about it, and before Aman and his
family knew about it too. So, they called Amrita and said,
'Please come home we need to talk to you.' She didn't know
what was going on, but she went home, and they confronted her
about it. And she just admitted everything. Like how she was
with another guy and that what they saw was real. And then she
said she didn't wanna marry Aman. That she just couldn't do it.
Like she just refused to marry him. Her parents were angry, and
tried to persuade her, and when she said no again, they told her
she *had* to. And Amrita just said she wouldn't and left and went
back to her uni house.

She came to mine the next day and told me what had happened.
Her parents kept calling her, but she just ignored them.

Beat.

And then a few days later her mum text her saying they wanted
to hear her out and asked her to come home so they could talk
about it. She was relieved to get that text. She wasn't sure how
it would work out where she didn't have to marry Aman and
could be with Rishi, but she also didn't wanna not talk to her
family... so she went home.

Beat.

I don't know much about what happened next. Whether they killed her as soon as she walked through the front door, or whether they actually did have a conversation and tried to work things out and then killed her if she still refused. It's weird, my feelings about it change all the time. Sometimes I think, 'Does it matter? I mean, she's still dead.' And then other times, I would give anything to know. I think it's the not knowing that keeps it with me. The not knowing is why I haven't been able to properly grieve, and move on, and get closure. Because I don't know what exactly I'm grieving other than my friend is dead. I don't know the details or the ins and outs, and maybe I don't wanna know them but right now it weirdly feels like it might help. I do know it was forced suicide. Her older brothers – cousins, but, you know, brothers. They locked her in a room with a rope. I know that. I guess at that point it was either she kills herself or they kill her. I think about her and that all the time. I think about how terrified she must've been in her final moments. How she probably begged, and cried, and screamed… but how they still made her do it. How they didn't open the door even though she was probably pounding on it. I think about the silence that came after that. That's probably how they knew she'd done it; there weren't any more cries or screams, and she wasn't banging on the door. There was nothing.

I'm not sure how my uni friends found out, but everyone text me to make sure I was okay. Atticus organised a pub thing for Amrita. I wasn't gonna go. I didn't have the energy to get dressed and talk to people. But then she was at every motive and as much as I didn't wanna go, it just felt wrong not going. So, I went.

MUSICIAN *plays 'Lag Jaa Gale' by Lata Mangeshkar on the acoustic guitar.*

I get to the pub and look around, and I can't see anyone. I walk round the tables and finally see Sam, Atticus, Jay, and lots of our other friends. I get hugged a lot. I get asked how I am a lot. I hate that question but always reply with the obligatory, 'I'm okay', with head nod and gentle smile. I make a bit of small talk but just kind of sit there really. My friend Priya asks if I want a drink. I don't but feel like I should and kinda wanna get away from the table, so I say yes. I'm at the bar. The bartender asks

me what I want, and there's just nothing I wanna drink. Gin and
lemonade doesn't feel right, I don't want beer or wine, I don't
want a Coke because I feel like I need some alcohol in me…
and then I clock the fridge.

Beat.

'I'll have a blue VK please'. (*Sips the VK.*) 'It's so disgusting' –
(*Chuckle.*) We sit back down, and I'm sat next to Jay. I haven't
said hi to him yet. He gives me a warm hug, and he goes to say
something and then sees my drink and is like 'Wow, blue VK?!'
'Yeah, it just felt right, you know?' We share a laugh and it's the
little ice-breaker I needed to feel somewhat comfortable tonight.
It looks like he's had a haircut recently because his fade is
immaculate. We talk about the football, whether sandwiches
should be cut down the middle or diagonally, and whether
cauliflower is a traditional Christmas vegetable. I think
sandwiches should be cut diagonally and he thinks they should
be cut down the middle, but shockingly we both agree that
cauliflower is not traditional. I wanna get some fresh air so
I step outside. I'm here for about five minutes when Jay comes
outside to see if I'm okay.

MUSICIAN *fades 'Lag Jaa Gale' into 'Tere Bin Nahin Lagda'.*

'Yeah, I'm okay', I say with head nod and gentle smile. He sits
down next to me and tells me that he's not okay. He tells me he
didn't know she was suicidal. He didn't know she was in that
much pain. If he knew he would have tried to help. 'I didn't
know either.' He's been talking it through with his dad a lot. His
dad's been telling him it's not his fault, but Jay can't accept that.
I kind of assumed his dad wasn't in his life. He tells me he feels
like a bad friend. He feels guilty.

Beat.

I've spoken to a few people tonight about Amrita and he's the
only one who feels the same as me even though he has no idea
what's actually happened. He understands, and he cares, and he
feels awful about it, and he'd do anything to make it right, and
he wishes so badly she was here, and he's so… articulate with
how he speaks even though grief is a really unmanageable
emotion, and he reminds me of her a bit, and he cares about
how I feel about everything, and he listens, and… and I'm

kissing him. It feels right, but it's not a good kiss. My lips are dry, and his breath kind of smells of beer which is… yeah. I pull away and… his lips are blue.

MUSICIAN *stops playing*.

At first, I panic and think he's really cold, but then I realise it's the VK.

Beat.

We just look at each other for a bit.

Beat.

I think we're both confused and… well I don't know about him but I kind of want it to happen again.

Long pause.

We're both just staring at each other. No one's saying anything and I hate awkward silences, but I can't think of a single thing to say.

Long pause.

It's getting uncomfortable at this point, and I can see him trying to think of something to say too but neither of us can manage it, and then finally he says, 'Did you know starfish don't have a brain?'

(*Looks around dumbfounded*.) 'What?'

He says it again: 'Did you know starfish don't have a brain?

(*Hesitantly*.) 'No, I – I didn't know that, Jay.'

Pause.

It's silent for a while again so I decide to head inside before he tells me another animal fact. I say bye to everyone and head home.

SIMRAN *moves the table in front of the chair.*

The next week or so was a strange one. I'm at Jay's flat. We've had a little nap; he's still asleep but I'm hungry so.

SIMRAN *starts making two sandwiches.*

One for me, one for him. We've been… hanging out… and stuff. And it's been nice. He makes me feel… comfortable and safe and… I'm just at ease around him. I don't ever feel like I have to fill silence when I'm with him. Like, I can just sit and exist in the same room as him, and that's enough. And he's kind and sweet and – and he bought oat milk for when I come round. And he cuts my sandwiches diagonally for me even though he thinks down the middle is the best. And he beefs me about Tottenham, but I don't even mind. If anything, I enjoy the flirty banter. The flanter. And he reminds me to make my fantasy team subs because I never remember, and I'm bottom of the league that I'm in. And – … And I've cut his sandwich down the middle.

Beat.

Ah – (*Exhale.*) fuck.

SIMRAN *thinks for a while. She goes to throw the sandwich in the bin. She stops. She looks at Jay. She puts the sandwich down in front of him.*

A few days later and I'm back at Jay's flat. He opens the door and teases me about catching feelings for him. He finds it hysterical. (*To Jay, mimicking.*) 'Oh hehehehe do one.' (*Grabs a mug from the table.*) I make a hot chocolate with oat milk. I don't like English tea, and I don't get how people do. The grip that bland, watery milk has on this country is unbelievable. And I don't like coffee; it's too bitter. Jay, the absolute psychopath, makes himself a black coffee and we start watching an episode of *Peep Show* – the one with Gerard's funeral – (*Sits.*) I've watched this show all the way through a few times, but I didn't know this was the next episode. I would've asked to watch something else if – there it is. He asks me how I'm feeling about Amrita's funeral.

Pause.

'Trying not to think about it really.'

Pause.

'Actually, maybe we should talk about it. My family's gonna be there too obviously and, erm, I think it's maybe best if we don't talk on Monday, maybe. Just because of my family, you know…?'

He's silent for a while. He asks me if I'm gonna talk to *anyone* at the funeral, or if it's just him I'm not gonna talk to.

Beat.

I know what he's saying. Which means he knows what I'm trying to say.

'Jay, we can talk, we just… I think it's best we don't talk a lot or on our own. It's just my family…'

He nods. He understands what I'm saying. He looks a bit ruined. I didn't know I could make someone look like that.

Beat.

'Do you want me to go? Okay.'

Stands up, moves the table upstage, and puts the mug on it.

'I'll see you on Monday.' He says 'Yeah. Won't speak to you though.'

I tell him I'm sorry. He just looks at me.

SIMRAN *leaves Jay's flat. She inhales and then exhales deeply. She stays here for a while, existing, thinking, breathing.*

'Lag Jaa Gale' by Lata Mangeshkar is played on the guitar and sung by the MUSICIAN. SIMRAN *takes off her hoodie and bottoms to reveal a simple white Indian outfit. She sits. The* MUSICIAN *stops playing.*

Jay and I don't talk for a few days. It's a slow few days. And then we're at the funeral. Me. Lots of my friends, my family. We're all here at the crematorium. Because, you know, she killed herself.

Knocking.

My dad knocks on the window and says I need to get out. I don't want to. I don't wanna leave the car because if I do then I'm actually at her funeral. If I leave the car, then it's real and I don't want it to be.

Knocking.

My dad knocks again. He's not the sort of guy to ask twice. (*Gets out of the car.*) It's boiling. I'm gonna get so dark standing in the sun like this. We join the queue –

Whilst in the queue she takes small steps in one direction. She stops when she sees Jay.

– and I see my friends queueing for the crematorium. I can't see Jay, though.

Beat.

About five minutes later Jay and some of our friends come out. He's wearing a black suit. Love a man in a suit. They walk towards us, and Jay and I catch eyes.

MUSICIAN *plays 'Tere Bin Nahin Lagda'.*

And we don't look away. We don't say hi or smile or anything we just look at each other, and he walks past me –

MUSICIAN *stops playing.*

SIMRAN *exhales loudly.*

That was louder than I would have liked it to be. My mum asks if I'm okay. 'Yeah, fine, just… emotional.'

SIMRAN *realises she hasn't been keeping up with the queue and moves to catch up.*

I'm near the front. Someone hands me flower petals and tells me to place them at the foot of Amrita's coffin. Her family are next to her coffin, dressed in white. Some are crying. Some aren't. I'm anxious to be close to them and I don't know what they're gonna say, but then I'm at Amrita's coffin and it's my turn to pay my respects.

MUSICIAN *plays 'Lag Jaa Gale'.*

I don't even realise I'm clenching my fists until I go to put the petals down. Am I meant to put them down one by one? All together? Does it matter where exactly I put them? Do I have to say something as I put them down? Am I meant to pray? I don't know. I don't know anything.

Long pause. SIMRAN stays looking at the coffin.

It's weird, I'm thinking of every memory we have together but at the same time I'm not thinking of anything. I'm holding up the queue, but I don't care. She was my friend.

Pause.

Okay, it's been too long now. Her dad's the first person I have to greet –

MUSICIAN *stops playing*.

I lock eyes with him, and my stomach turns. I have to hug her dad. It's weird if I don't. I place my arms as gently as possible around him because a tight hug equals forgiveness or I like him or something. I don't know if that's the worst five seconds of my life or if the hug with her mum or her brothers is. Right, I've greeted them all. I'm done.

SIMRAN *collects herself in the fresh air outside*.

I enter the service room with my family. I see Jay. He's got a seat near the back with some friends. He doesn't see me, but the back of his head looks so good. I sit down with my family near the front. (*Stands and turns*.) Amrita's family enters. I catch eyes with Jay –

MUSICIAN *plays 'Tere Bin Nahin Lagda'*.

We hold each other's gaze for what feels like forever. But it's a good forever.

Sits. MUSICIAN *stops playing*.

I listen to speeches from Amrita's family. About how devastated they are and how they would do anything to have her back. And I swear to God I've never felt anger like it. I see Aman. I recognise him from photos. I don't really know what to do, I just get even more angry. He makes me think about Rishi. He's not here, obviously. I hope he's okay.

A moment of SIMRAN *allowing herself to be angry and upset*.

My dad puts an arm around me. And he leans into my ear, and he whispers, 'Don't worry, you wouldn't be so stupid.' And I just freeze. I don't even look at him… I just look down. I want his arm off me, but I can't move. I feel like I can't breathe, like my lungs literally won't expand like they should. Eventually he takes his arm off and – (*Deep breath*.) oxygen flows – (*A few more*.) Finally, the service is over – (*Stands*.)

I walk outside and hear someone call my name. It's Atticus. I smile at him gently and give him a hug. Jay is with him. I give him a hug. I shouldn't, but I do. It's a quick one but with the tightest squeeze you could imagine. We don't say anything to each other. I say bye to everyone and go with my family to Amrita's family's house. Arun gets me a plate with some pakore on. (*Sits and puts the plate down.*) I've never wanted to be anywhere less.

Beat.

Did they lock her in this room and make her do it? Or was it upstairs in her bedroom? It was somewhere in this house so I'm just a bit confused as to why we're all just sat here? I just… I feel like I'm going crazy. Like I'm the only one who's struggling with this concept.

(*Stands.*) We finally go home.

SIMRAN *takes off her Indian outfit, grabs a loofah from her suitcase, steps into the shower, and starts scrubbing. A shower sound effect plays.* MUSICIAN *sings the Gayatri Mantra whilst* SIMRAN *undresses to her underwear.*

I get straight in the shower, and I start scrubbing like you wouldn't believe. Like this was low-key a workout. I feel so unclean from having to hug her family. I'm trying to scrub away the hugs but I'm also thinking about what my dad said to me and maybe that means my mum did know what would happen when she told Amrita's parents, and I think about my brother. I don't know if he knows what actually happened but if he does he must be so so sad because he didn't know what he was doing and I run out of energy or willpower or… (*Stands panting, crying.*) It isn't until I get really hot and feel like I could pass out that I get out.

Shower sound stops.

MUSICIAN *starts singing the Gayatri Mantra again.*

SIMRAN *takes a sweatshirt and the original bottoms she was wearing out of her suitcase and puts them on. She plaits her hair.*

It's like six p.m., but I don't care. I'm done for the day.

Lights dim. MUSICIAN *sings and plays 'Lag Jaa Gale' on the guitar.* SIMRAN *sits, closes her eyes, and takes deep breaths. She checks her phone once. She disappointedly puts it down. The mood is sombre, reflective, and exhausted.*

The lights come back up.

SIMRAN *changes her sweatshirt to the original top she was wearing.*

It's a few days after the funeral. I'm outside Jay's flat. We haven't really spoken, just a few texts yesterday.

Jay opens the door.

'Hey.'

Pause.

'How are you?' He tells me he's okay.

Long pause. Uncomfortable.

'Did you know that polar bears actually have black skin?'

Beat.

He asks me if that means my family don't like polar bears.

'No, I think they're pretty... indifferent about pol– '

Beat.

'I'm sorry. I put you in a difficult position, and I'm sorry. I've been thinking about Monday a lot and I didn't think about how you might have needed me. I'm sorry. I'm here now if you do...'

SIMRAN *enters the flat.*

'I've missed you.' He doesn't say anything back. (*Sits.*) 'Jay, I don't think you realise what I'm willing to risk here.'

Pause.

'I'm risking dating someone my family won't like... But I'm willing to – not willing – I *want* to. It's been a really shit few weeks, and you've anchored me through it. And I really care about you. And I have energy for you. I don't have energy for other people. I'm so tired, Jay. Like... like my spirit is tired, you know? But I can't sleep. And I'm either not hungry at all or I am hungry but I'm too tired to make something, so either way I don't eat. And I couldn't tell you the last time I laughed. That's how I've been, and I still found the energy to see you. I care. And I'm sorry. And I think I need you to keep going because I don't have energy for anyone or anything else.'

He nods. He kisses me. He cares. He doesn't say it, but I can tell he cares. Probably not the healthiest way to start a relationship, but, you know what, only the baddest of bitches are that dependent on another person.

SIMRAN*'s smile fades and she looks at audience members. Sonder.*

Yeah… any problems I give them don't make mine feel smaller right now.

I mean I'm on a train – I'm on a train to fucking City Airport to move to Edinburgh with my boyfriend because they know. Because my family know and neither of us are safe. Some – some lady who knows my parents saw us out together last month and told them and now they know, and they are up the wall. They are humiliated and embarrassed and ashamed and angry and… 'You wouldn't be so stupid.'

Beat.

I'm at my uni flat and I get a call from Arun. He never calls me. I answer and he starts whispering something really fast. I can't hear him or understand him, so I tell him to speak up. He says 'I can't, I'm scared they'll hear me. I'll Snap you, don't save the messages.' I say 'Okay' and hang up. He Snaps me, I open the messages. I start to read them, and then I see the phrase 'You were in Hackney on Friday with a Black guy.'

SIMRAN *scans the message over and over, faster and faster. She drops her phone. She stares at it. She picks it back up.*

'There's a lady in the living room with Mum and Dad and she's told them you were in Hackney on Friday with a Black guy, and they seem really angry.' His room is right above the living room so he can hear everything. I message him back and say 'Are you sure that's what she said?' He says 'Yes.' I ask who the lady is, he says he didn't recognise her. I tell him I love him and that if they ask, he has to say he doesn't know anything. He has to act confused, he has to act like he has no idea what they're talking about. He says 'Okay.' I call Jay.

Answerphone message plays.

I call again.

Answerphone message plays again.

I spam his fucking phone with calls and texts and finally – 'Jay.
You need to pack a bag and stay at a friend's place for a while.
I haven't been totally honest with you. My parents have found
out about us. They're really angry. They could hurt us. I can
explain properly later. You just need to pack a bag and go.' He's
confused and annoyed and he's aski– 'Please, please just do it.
Okay?' He's still really confused and is being kind of
aggressive, but he agrees. 'I love you.' He doesn't say it back.

'Hey, Sam! No chance I can stay at yours tonight is there?
Awesome, thanks. Yeah, yeah, all good. See you in a bit.'

SIMRAN *starts frantically packing the suitcase.*

I'll tell her when I get there. Maybe. Probably missing all the
essentials but I just need to get out this flat.

I leg it to the station and jump on the train.

SIMRAN *sits down, breathless and riddled with anxiety.*

The Tube is boiling. I can feel my body sweating – I don't know
if it's anxiety or the heat. I'm looking around the half-empty
carriage, looking for my family or someone, anyone I might
know, or who might know me. No one. The train reaches its
first stop. I stare at the open doors waiting to see who comes on.
No one I know. I'm trying to calm myself down, but I don't
know how. And then I see the woman sat across from me. She's
wearing a floral green dress and flats. And there's a bit of toilet
paper stuck to the bottom of her left shoe. We reach the next
stop, the doors open, and I don't look up. I'm transfixed on this
toilet paper, and how the fresh air makes it move. It looks like
it's dancing or trying to escape. Did it just get attached on the
street? Was she in the bathroom and it got stuck? Or maybe it's
a fashion statement, I don't know. Maybe she was in the
bathroom at work, and it got stuck. Yeah, I think that's it.

SIMRAN*'s breathing has calmed now.*

Beat.

My phone buzzes and I'm back. I'm not looking at the toilet roll
any more. I grab my phone and see a few missed calls from my
parents. (*Breathing intensifies again.*)

Beat. SIMRAN *puts her phone down.*

I wonder what she does. Receptionist? Yeah, let's go with that.
I wonder what happened for her today, what problems she has.
Well, I'm staring at one. She's got toilet roll stuck to her shoe.
(*Her breathing calms.*) Maybe... maybe she went on a date
after work, and it didn't go well and now she's going home.
Yeah, that's it. I go back to my phone, turn Find My Friends off,
turn Snap Maps off, block their numbers. She crosses her legs
and sees the toilet roll. She takes it off – I guess it wasn't a
fashion statement, then. The train reaches my stop. I don't get
off. I wait until the next stop and then get off. I guess for safety
it's best to mislead them and go to a different station, right?

I get to Sam's flat. She asks me what's wrong. I don't know
where to begin, I don't know whether I should tell her or not.
I don't. I just tell her I've fallen out with my flatmates and can't
stay there any more and didn't wanna live with Jay just yet. She
nods and... there I am. Hiding there.

SIMRAN *opens her suitcase.*

I call Jay that night. He asks every question and I give him
every answer. Truthfully. I tell him I was just trying to protect
him. He doesn't believe me. He's fuming. I tell him I love him.
He doesn't say it back. I tell him I'm scared and that I need to
hear it. He says it. He doesn't mean it, but he says it. And then
he hangs up.

I call him again two days later. I tell him I'm scared, I'm
fucking scared they're gonna find me. He tells me to calm down
and that it'll be okay. That we just need to wait it out. I tell him
it won't, I know it won't. We need to leave, we're not safe in
London. He asks where I'd like to go. I don't... Ed-Edinburgh?
It's far away and seems cool. And Scottish people are meant to
be really funny aren't they. He says 'Okay, if being there will
make you feel safer, okay.' We hang up and I book two tickets
for Thursday morning.

Lights down and up.

SIMRAN *finishes packing her suitcase and closes it.*

It took me ages to fall asleep last night. And it took me ages to
get out of bed this morning. I don't know why because I need to

leave London. But it did. The only thing that got me out of bed was my bladder. Classic. I text Jay 'Good morning' earlier – he's not replied yet. Probably doing some last-minute packing too. I can't wait to see him. (*Picks up the piece of toast.*) That'll do. And I'm gone. I walk to the station, hop on the train, and here we are at... (*Looks around.*) Canning Town Station.

A moment or two of SIMRAN *existing in the present.*

Train door beeping.

(*Something catches her attention.*) Someone's bag's caught in the door. Fuck's sake. Right, not being funny. You see the flashing lights, you hear the beeps. The door is going to close so unless you're agile and fast, don't jump for it. I don't know why there's people built like sumo wrestlers jumping for the train. Another train *will be here* in two minutes.

The only way to get here was through Shadwell. That stop was the worst minute of my life. I put a facemask on – (*Holds it up.*) I don't even care about that any more but anything to not be seen.

We never got a proper goodbye when everything happened. And I know it's only been a week but so much has gone on. I'm so excited to see this boy. Although, at this point, I kind of wish Amrita had introduced me to an Indian guy.

Beat.

(*Quietly to herself whilst looking at audience members.*) Why they're on the train, where they're going and why, where they live, what job they have, who their friends and family are, what problems they have...

City Airport Station announcement. SIMRAN *reaches her stop.*

This is me.

She exits the train with her suitcase.

We said we'd meet at the gate, so I go through security – I get randomly selected – and I walk to the gate.

(*Looking for him among the audience members.*) He's not here yet.

SIMRAN *sits there waiting. She checks her phone. She looks around. A boarding announcement for a flight to Edinburgh is heard. She looks for Jay. This should be painfully long.*

A final boarding announcement plays.

SIMRAN *looks for Jay.*

MUSICIAN *plays 'Tere Bin Nahin Lagda' on guitar.*

Slow fade to black.

End.

HOW WE BEGIN

Elisabeth Lewerenz

For Clara,
who showed me how wonderful it is
to be loved out in the open

ELISABETH LEWERENZ

Elisabeth Lewerenz is a playwright and performer hailing from Bonn, Germany. She developed her first scenes and short plays for the Bonn University Shakespeare Company, one of which earned her a nomination for Best Original Play at the 2018 FEATS Festival in Antwerp, Belgium. She was then chosen as one of only six participants for the VAULT New Writers Programme in 2019. The eight-week playwriting course, led by Camilla Whitehill, culminated in a sold-out showcase in March that year. Elisabeth's first full-length play *How We Begin* had work-in-progress showing at the King's Head Theatre in August 2019, as part of their Queer Season. Back in her hometown, she was commissioned to develop a play to commemorate the 250th anniversary of Beethoven's birth – *The Silenced Symphony* was part of the Edinburgh Fringe's digital programming in August 2021. In October 2022, Elisabeth performed their first German-language solo show *Fremdkörper*, which deals with themes of sex education and the relationship with one's own body, to a sold-out house at the Brotfabrik Bühne Bonn, with more performances planned for 2023. Elisabeth also regularly performs as drag king Willie Eyelash across venues in her home state of North-Rhine Westphalia.

How We Begin was first performed at VAULT Festival on 14 February 2023, with the following cast:

HELEN   Talia Pick
DIANA   Emma Lucia

Director   Elizabeth Benbow
Producer   Antonia Georgieva

Characters

HELEN
DIANA

Note on Text

A forward slash (/) indicates the point of interruption.

HELEN *and* DIANA *stand next to each other.*

HELEN. It begins during freshers' week.

We are paired together for this trust-fall thing. I reach out –

She reaches for DIANA *with her left arm.*

DIANA. I reach out

She reaches for HELEN *with her right arm. They lean away from each other slightly, fingers almost meeting.*

HELEN. And my fingers thread into yours.

DIANA. No, my fingers thread into yours.

HELEN. Fingers were threaded, let's leave it at that.

DIANA. The important thing is

HELEN. The important thing is

My hands have never found another pair of hands so easily before.

DIANA. And you're with someone.

HELEN. And you're with someone.

And I don't even know I'm into women yet.

DIANA. Can you imagine?

You, a heterosexual?

HELEN. Me, straight.

It begins three years later.

And I'm in Italy.

DIANA. Year abroad.

HELEN. It's three years later.

DIANA. We've been friends for three years.

HELEN. And we don't see each other all that often.

DIANA. Hard with you in Italy.

HELEN. Hard with you back home.

It's three years later and I'm in Italy and we Skype.

DIANA. Because I haven't heard from you.

HELEN. Because I haven't heard from you.

And it feels like I'm on a first date with my laptop.

DIANA. That's ridiculous.

HELEN. You're ridiculous.

There's this flutter in my stomach.

And I think

I hope she thinks I'm cool.

DIANA. I hope she thinks I'm cool?

It's been three years. If I didn't think you were cool, I wouldn't Skype with you.

Also

HELEN. Yeah?

DIANA. No one is cool on Skype.

HELEN. And we talk.

DIANA. And we talk.

HELEN. And we talk.

DIANA. And we talk.

HELEN. You get the gist.

We talk.

DIANA. We talk.

HELEN. A lot.

DIANA. But not enough.

HELEN. Never enough.

DIANA. And you're cool, even on Skype.

HELEN. Maybe I should've known then.

DIANA. How are you cool on Skype?

HELEN. It's a gift.

DIANA. It begins another year later.

HELEN. And I'm back home.

DIANA. And I've never left.

And I'm with someone.

HELEN. And I'm not. Not any more.

Instead, I'm kissing tons of people.

DIANA. Tons.

HELEN. Legions.

DIANA. Most of your friends.

HELEN. So many people.

DIANA. But not me.

HELEN. You're with someone.

DIANA. I'm with someone.

HELEN. But not with me.

At least I figured out I'm not straight.

DIANA. And we start to spend more time together.

HELEN. We see each other everywhere.

DIANA. I'm disappointed if I don't see you when I'm at a party.

HELEN. I'm disappointed if I leave before you get there.

DIANA. We never get there at the same time.

HELEN. We never leave at the same time.

DIANA. I'm disappointed when I miss you.

HELEN. And I miss you a lot.

DIANA. There's that one time when we say goodbye.

HELEN. I'm sat on a chair and you want to hug me from behind.

So I turn around like this.

She turns around.

DIANA. And I bend down like this.

She bends down. They're bent at weird angles, next to each other.

And I swear I just want to kiss you on the cheek.

HELEN. I just want to kiss you on the cheek.

DIANA. But because of my angle

HELEN. Because of my timing, my mouth lands

DIANA. On my mouth.

I apologise.

HELEN. I apologise.

There's nothing to apologise for.

DIANA. How did we not notice?

HELEN. I honestly don't know.

They come out of their weird angles.

DIANA. It begins three months later.

And I'm in your flat.

It's midnight.

HELEN. It's past midnight.

DIANA. We're on your sofa.

HELEN. Talking about relationships.

DIANA. And how you don't like them.

HELEN. About how hard you have to work for love.

DIANA. I'm with someone.

HELEN. I'm still not with someone.

And I don't kiss as many people any more.

DIANA. Only the occasional people.

But I'm with someone.

HELEN. And you love him.

DIANA. I love him a lot.

HELEN. But you say there's someone else you're in love with.

DIANA. Do you not know then?

HELEN. Me?

No

But –

DIANA. But?

HELEN. But I hope then.

And I hope I'm not wrong.

DIANA. And I say

HELEN. Something really great

You say

DIANA. Are you prepared for me to make this awkward?

HELEN. And I am

So unprepared

DIANA. I say

It's you

HELEN. Me

DIANA. It's you I'm in love with.

HELEN. And I say –

Long pause.

That's what I say.

DIANA. And then you curl up in my arms.

HELEN. Because my eyes can't meet yours but your limbs meet my limbs just fine.

DIANA. This is fine.

HELEN. Fine

I say

DIANA. You say you want to say something.

HELEN. But what comes out is –

Long pause.

DIANA. Until you say

HELEN. Until I say

I've loved you for so long it's become a kind of background noise.

And if this is something you want

I'm here.

DIANA. You're here.

HELEN. With you.

DIANA. With me.

HELEN. And –

DIANA. And?

HELEN. And –

DIANA. And –

HELEN. I really need to go to the toilet so badly.

DIANA. Way to kill the mood.

HELEN. But then I count to three with kisses on your skin.

DIANA. One

HELEN. Lands on your shoulder.

DIANA. Two

HELEN. Lands on your neck.

DIANA. Three

HELEN. Lands on your mouth.

DIANA. It begins right there.

HELEN. It begins right here.

They look at each other.

—

HELEN. This is how it ends.

It's two a.m. when I kiss you goodbye.

We're standing at my doorstep and it's dark outside and really cold. I'm not wearing too many clothes at this point but I don't care. It's good actually, being outside in the cold, because I'm hot all over.

DIANA. You are hot all over.

HELEN. Not in that way, more in like a 'fuck I'm really sweaty and I probably don't smell all that nice and my make-up is definitely more than half gone at this point so it's bound to look a bit... interesting'. I look like that.

DIANA. You look lovely.

HELEN. No, I don't.

DIANA. You do, you look sort of –

HELEN. What?

DIANA. Ravaged.

HELEN. Is ravaged code for 'a bit shit but in a nice way'?

DIANA. No, it's code for 'Would you please believe me when I tell you you look good?'

HELEN. Alright.

It's two a.m. when I kiss you goodbye.

DIANA. And it just instantly feels weird not to be where you are.

HELEN. For some reason, it feels weird not to see you.

While I take off what's left of my make-up –

DIANA. I ride home on my bike.

HELEN. While I finally exhale –

DIANA. I inhale and step through the front door.

HELEN. He'll be asleep though, won't he?

DIANA. Yeah.

Yeah, he'll be asleep.

HELEN. While I notice that you left your phone on my coffee table –

DIANA. I notice that I left my phone on your coffee table.

HELEN. For a hot second I think I should call and let you know that you left your phone on my coffee table.

DIANA. Wow.

HELEN. I blame you.

DIANA. Me?

HELEN. How am I supposed to think straight when it's two in the morning and I just slept with my best friend?

DIANA. Fair point.

While I tiptoe around the flat –

HELEN. I realise that calling you is not very productive.

And I open my emails on my phone to message you.

I write…

Hey.

DIANA *laughs*.

What?

DIANA. Nothing… just… hey.

HELEN. Too casual?

DIANA. You just had your fingers inside of me.

Beat.

HELEN. I write…

Sweet cheeks,

DIANA. You do?

HELEN. No, of course not, I write

Babe,

I don't want to assume anything but I guess you leaving your phone here is part of a cunning plan to see me again tomorrow. Let me know when you want to pick it up?

And I sign it bye because just saying 'bye' sounds like you're announcing your sexuality to everyone every time you leave a room.

DIANA. Bi.

HELEN. Bi.

DIANA. Bi-bi.

HELEN. And not just any bi.

DIANA. Good-bi.

HELEN. A very good-bi to you.

DIANA. It's silly.

HELEN. You had to have been there.

I sign it bye. Not even my name, just bye.

While I smile like an idiot –

DIANA. I read your email on my laptop.

And I smile like an idiot.

And I reply.

I write…

Babe,

You've seen right through me. I'll pick it up around nine?

HELEN *makes a face*.

Ten?

HELEN. Do you realise it's two in the morning?

DIANA. I'll pick it up around twelve.

HELEN. And you sign your email –

They look at each other. They don't say it, just have a quiet chuckle.

While I go to bed –

DIANA. I go to bed.

HELEN. While I set my alarm –

DIANA. I'm trying to get my brain to shut up.

HELEN. While I go through what just happened –

DIANA. My brain will not shut up at all.

HELEN. While I lie down –

DIANA. I have to nudge him slightly to get under the covers.

HELEN. Tomorrow, just before you get here, I'm going to wonder if this was just something you needed to get out of your system.

Just before you get here, I'm going to wonder what this is going to do to our friendship.

Just before you get here, I'm going to make a mental list of all the friends I've kissed that I'm still friends with.

DIANA. Tomorrow, what's going to happen is this.

—

HELEN. There?

DIANA. Yes.

HELEN. There?

DIANA. Yes.

HELEN. What about there?

DIANA *laughs*.

What?

DIANA. This is insane.

HELEN. There.

DIANA *makes a pleased sound*.

DIANA. You're good at this.

HELEN. Thank you.

DIANA *makes a ridiculous sound*.

HELEN *laughs*.

DIANA. Sorry.

HELEN. No, no, no, don't be.

DIANA. It's just what I sound like.

HELEN. I love it.

DIANA. Sorry.

HELEN. No, seriously, I'm enjoying this.

DIANA makes another ridiculous sound.

HELEN smiles to herself.

DIANA makes another ridiculous sound.

DIANA. Let me?

HELEN. Sure.

HELEN starts breathing heavily.

DIANA. Like this?

HELEN. Yeah.

More breathing.

DIANA. There?

HELEN. Not so fast.

DIANA. Okay.

HELEN is slightly uncomfortable.

What?

HELEN. I'm sorry.

DIANA. What is it?

HELEN. I should've told you before we did this.

DIANA. What?

HELEN. It's your nails.

DIANA. Fuck.

HELEN. They're a bit… long.

DIANA. Sorry.

HELEN. You've got straight-girl nails.

DIANA. I'm so sorry.

HELEN. It's okay.

Beat.

DIANA. I'm going to ask him tomorrow.

HELEN. Oh yeah?

DIANA. Yeah.

HELEN. You know you don't have to.

DIANA. I know. But I want to.

HELEN. Okay.

    If that's what you want.

DIANA. It is.

    It's the best way to do it.

HELEN. Okay.

    Beat.

DIANA. Next time.

    I'll cut my nails next time.

    Beat.

HELEN. Next time.

—

DIANA. This is how it ends.

    My boyfriend is very…

HELEN. Assured.

DIANA. Confident.

    He's very…

HELEN. Adult.

DIANA. Serious.

    He's very…

HELEN. Male.

    A look.

    I'm sorry, he just is, he's very…

DIANA. Yeah.

    Not male in a very male way.

    He's not like

HELEN. These are my muscles.

DIANA. Not like

HELEN. I haven't looked in a mirror since 2012.

DIANA. Not like

HELEN. My penis – is very manly.

DIANA. He's not like that.

HELEN. He's not very tall.

DIANA. He uses concealer to hide the bags under his eyes.

HELEN. He's the one who introduced gender-neutral language in his office.

DIANA. He's a good guy.

HELEN. But anytime I see him, I just always think he's very –

DIANA. Male, I get it.

He's his own person. And he doesn't mind me being my own person. We can be our own people together.

It's Sunday night when I ask him.

HELEN. Sunday night is your date night.

DIANA. I ask him –

Would you mind if I slept with other people?

Beat.

HELEN. Do you –

Do you usually ask him stuff like that in that tone of voice?

DIANA. What tone of voice?

HELEN. Like you just asked him what kind of pasta he wants for dinner?

DIANA. I guess.

HELEN. Oh.

DIANA. I ask him –

Would you mind if I slept with other people?

And I'm a bit surprised when he goes

HELEN. Yes.

DIANA. I go…

Why?

He says –

HELEN. If you sleep with other people, I'll have to sleep with other people.

DIANA. And I go…

I mean, if that's what you want, then that's –

HELEN. I don't want to sleep with other people, I just think if you do –

DIANA. Yeah?

HELEN. I kind of have to.

Beat.

Otherwise there's this…

Beat.

Imbalance.

DIANA. He doesn't ask

HELEN. Are you sleeping with other people?

DIANA. He doesn't ask

HELEN. Who are you sleeping with?

DIANA. He doesn't ask

HELEN. Is it someone I know?

DIANA. He says

HELEN. Goodnight. I love you.

—

DIANA. I'm sorry.

HELEN. It's fine.

To be honest, I didn't expect him to be all open about it.

For what it's worth.

I enjoyed those two days, babe.

No hard feelings.

Obviously.

DIANA. Wait.

Are you breaking up with me?

HELEN. I thought you were breaking up with me.

DIANA. I'm not breaking up with you.

HELEN. You're not?

DIANA. Of course not.

I mean

If this means you're out, I respect that.

But I'm not going to stop just because I don't have my boyfriend's approval.

That's not me.

HELEN. Wow.

DIANA. Is that a good wow?

HELEN. That's a very impressed wow.

DIANA. Look.

HELEN. Imagine me waving pompons around while I say wow.

DIANA. We shouldn't be having this conversation over text.

HELEN. Well, we are anyway.

At two in the morning.

What is it about us and two in the morning?

DIANA. I would have liked to do this out in the open.

I really would have liked to be the eccentric hip bohemian person arriving at the party with two partners.

Believe me, I would have loved to parade you around.

And I don't want you to feel like you have to hide anything.

But the way I see it.

More love is always a good thing.

HELEN. More love is always a good thing.

DIANA. So we're doing this?

—

HELEN. I like this.

DIANA. I like kissing you in dark corners.

HELEN. I like pressing you up against walls.

DIANA. I like messing with your hair.

HELEN. I like wearing stuff I know you will like.

DIANA. I like how I can tell when an outfit is for me.

HELEN. I like how your leg feels against mine when I put it there.

DIANA. I like how you've worked out that I love it when you bite my lip.

HELEN. I like the sound you make when I bite your lip.

DIANA. I like this part of your neck.

HELEN. I like how your back looks when you lie on my bed.

DIANA. I like your belly.

HELEN. Your left ear.

DIANA. Your forehead.

HELEN. I think I'd like your internal organs if I could see them.

DIANA. Your right ear.

HELEN. Hell, I'm just gonna go there, I like your internal organs.

DIANA. I like that I don't have to worry about what underwear I'm wearing.

HELEN. I like that I don't have to worry about how hairy my armpits are.

DIANA. I like that thing you do when we say goodbye.

HELEN. What thing?

DIANA. You know.

> DIANA *stretches her arm out and wiggles with her fingers.*

> That thing.

> When I leave, you always go –

> DIANA *repeats the same gesture.*

> Like you want me to come back but also wave goodbye.

> DIANA *repeats the same gesture.*

> HELEN *copies her.*

HELEN. Really?

DIANA. Yes!

HELEN. Don't make fun of me.

DIANA. I'm not.

HELEN. I'm very vulnerable.

DIANA. I like – this is going to sound horrible.

HELEN. Go on.

DIANA. I like that it makes me feel –

> I mean, you make me feel really –

HELEN. Yeah?

DIANA. Queer.

> Is that bad?

HELEN. No.

> No, that's not bad at all.

—

HELEN. This is how it ends.

> It's Saturday and we're at this birthday party.

DIANA. Fay's birthday. And she's booked a table at the same bar that we all inevitably book a table at for our birthdays.

> It's the first time we're with our friends since this whole thing started.

HELEN. It's the first time and it's just stupidly easy.

I'm sitting next to you.

DIANA. I'm sitting next to you.

HELEN. And it feels a bit… mischievous almost.

I hold your hand under the table.

No one takes a second glance.

DIANA. I lean on you.

Nobody notices.

HELEN. There's a lot of…

DIANA. Touching.

HELEN. Not touching touching, more like…

I put my arm next to yours on the table.

DIANA. And our arms touch at the side, here.

Upper arm.

HELEN. Lower arm.

DIANA. And shoulder.

HELEN. Just for good measure.

No one minds.

DIANA. I cross my right foot over your left foot.

No one sees.

HELEN. We're all tangled up in each other.

I mean, people are blind.

DIANA. And stupid.

HELEN. People are, occasionally, blind and stupid.

Beat.

Maybe it's because our friends are pretty, you know…

DIANA. Touchy-feely?

HELEN (*overlapping*). Straight?

Yeah, touchy-feely.

They're used to people being close.

DIANA. Physically close.

HELEN. Without thinking anything of it.

DIANA. You know what, no. That can't be it.

HELEN. Why not?

DIANA. Do you remember Fay and Arthur?

HELEN. Yeah?

DIANA. There was that period of time, when Arthur still had that girlfriend, but you'd see him and Fay together everywhere. And everyone was all over it. For weeks it was all, 'Did you see them talking at the bar? Did you seem them arriving at that party together? Did you see them existing in the same room at the same time?'

HELEN. Oh, you're right.

DIANA. See?

HELEN. They don't talk about us like that.

DIANA. Eventually, between all the chatter and the gins and the tonics, we sneak off.

No one wonders where we went.

HELEN. And it's nice.

DIANA. Sneaking off into a corner.

HELEN. The music is loud.

DIANA. You're dressed up.

HELEN. I put in a bit of effort.

DIANA. For Fay.

HELEN. Not strictly speaking for Fay.

DIANA. You look…

HELEN. Yeah?

DIANA. You look…

HELEN. What?

DIANA. Actually I can't see you very well, it's really dark in there.

HELEN. Fuck off.

DIANA. I know you look beautiful.

HELEN. How?

DIANA. I just do.

HELEN. When we get back, no one asks where we've been.

DIANA. No one thinks about analysing our every move.

It's not like Fay and Arthur.

HELEN. God, Fay and Arthur, that was wild.

DIANA. Right?

HELEN. Yeah.

I remember because your boyfriend, after weeks of everyone speculating, just went up to them and said, square in their face: Are you two sleeping together?

Beat. Then DIANA *laughs.*

DIANA. He did, didn't he?

HELEN. Yeah. He did.

It's Saturday and we leave Fay's birthday together.

DIANA. Although we didn't come together.

HELEN. Well –

DIANA. Don't.

HELEN. We didn't come together – yet.

DIANA *facepalms.*

DIANA. What did I just say?

HELEN. You love it.

DIANA. No.

HELEN. Secretly. Secretly, you love it.

HELEN *looks at* DIANA. *Beat.*

DIANA. Secretly.

—

HELEN. On my doorstep.

DIANA. In your kitchen while the kettle boils.

HELEN. On my sofa.

DIANA. In your living room, sort of…

HELEN. Spinning.

DIANA. In your bed.

HELEN. In the bathroom at that hipstery bar.

DIANA. In the bathroom at that housewarming party.

HELEN. In Berlin.

DIANA. Oh, everywhere in Berlin.

HELEN. When we did that weekend away?

DIANA. Everywhere in Berlin.

HELEN. In our hotel bed.

DIANA. At that terrible Indian restaurant.

HELEN. At breakfast.

DIANA. In front of the Berlin Wall.

HELEN. Is that offensive?

DIANA. I'm not sure.

HELEN. At the Brandenburger Tor.

DIANA. I bet it's offensive.

HELEN. It's not not offensive.

DIANA. At every red light.

HELEN. In every elevator.

DIANA. On every escalator.

HELEN. At the airport, queueing at security.

DIANA. I bet everyone really hated us.

HELEN. So what, straight couples kiss in public all the time.

DIANA. At the gate.

HELEN. In the plane.

DIANA. At passport control.

> HELEN *wants to make the next point but can't. They stopped kissing at passport control.*

—

HELEN. There?

DIANA. No.

HELEN. There?

DIANA. No.

HELEN. There?

DIANA. Yes.

HELEN. Really?

DIANA. Wait, no.

HELEN. Fuck.

DIANA. What about here?

HELEN. That's in three weeks.

DIANA. I know.

HELEN. And I'll be on my period.

DIANA. That's literally the first night where I don't have plans yet.

HELEN. Fuck it, let's do that then.

DIANA. Okay.

> I'm really sorry.

HELEN. It's okay, I've got stuff to do as well.

DIANA. It's a really long time.

HELEN. I'll see you at the brunch thing on Sunday.

DIANA. Yeah but…

HELEN. I know.

Beat.

DIANA. What about…

No.

HELEN. Go on.

DIANA. I'm not sure you'll like it.

HELEN. Am I going to like it less than not seeing you for three weeks?

DIANA. How about if we meet before work?

Silence.

HELEN. Before what now?

DIANA. I'm serious.

HELEN. I start working at nine.

DIANA. Yes.

HELEN. I have to leave the house at eight.

DIANA. Yes.

HELEN. Do you see where I'm going with this?

DIANA. Look, I think it's either going to be this or in three weeks.

HELEN. I know.

I know.

I just –

I love my bed.

DIANA. I know.

HELEN. I like sleep.

DIANA. I know.

HELEN.

DIANA.

HELEN.

DIANA.

HELEN. So should we say, like, seven?

—

DIANA. This is how it ends.

When you open the door, you say –

HELEN. It's too early for this.

DIANA. Too early for what?

HELEN. Life.

DIANA. I brought coffee.

HELEN. You put the coffee down.

And you don't waste a second, you say –

DIANA. Do we have time?

You say –

HELEN. We don't have long.

DIANA. But then you say –

HELEN. But I'm willing to try.

And –

HELEN *laughs*.

DIANA. What?

HELEN. I've never seen someone undress so quickly before.

DIANA. A trail of clothes leads from the hall to your bedroom.

HELEN. Your sweater.

DIANA. Your pyjama bottoms.

HELEN. Your jeans.

DIANA. Your T-shirt.

HELEN. Your bra.

DIANA. Your pants.

HELEN. Your pants.

DIANA. Your bra.

HELEN. Twenty minutes later I'm in the bathroom, putting make-up on as fast as I can, thinking thank God I didn't put any on before you got here.

DIANA. Twenty minutes later, I'm lying in your sheets, examining the stack of books next to your bed.

HELEN. Thirty minutes later, I'm wondering where my socks went.

DIANA. Thirty minutes later, I'm wondering why you've got *The Adventures of Sherlock Holmes* next to your bed.

HELEN. Thirty-three minutes later, I find my socks under your jeans.

DIANA. Thirty-three minutes later, I've read the first three pages of *The Adventures of Sherlock Holmes*.

HELEN. Thirty-five minutes later, I tell you to get out of bed, I need to go to work.

DIANA. Thirty-five minutes later, you're back in bed, reading me two more pages of *The Adventures of Sherlock Holmes* while you lie on my stomach.

HELEN. Forty minutes later I do actually kick you out and then I kick myself out after you, take the coffee and say that I haven't had breakfast yet.

DIANA. Forty minutes later I complain that you didn't tell me, I would've brought you breakfast.

HELEN. Forty minutes later I'm doing all I can not to make a joke about having pussy for breakfast.

HELEN *takes a sip of coffee.*

DIANA. That's gone cold, hasn't it?

HELEN. Yeah.

—

DIANA. Seventeen. Or something.

HELEN. Seventeen?

DIANA. Maybe eighteen. Mum and Dad's anniversary. They have this friend, Maureen, who lives abroad, so they don't see her that often but she was in the country for their anniversary and she brought her girlfriend. I thought it was just a friend of hers at first but then I saw them kissing in the line for the buffet.

HELEN. Wow.

DIANA. So yeah, I think seventeen. That was the first time I saw two women kiss in real life.

HELEN. That's mad.

DIANA. What about you?

HELEN. I don't know.

DIANA. Well, what a great story.

HELEN. Sorry, my brain just shuts down after midnight.

DIANA. Do you want me to go?

HELEN. No, stay, I'm awake.

But I genuinely don't know. It was probably just two drunk girls kissing at a freshers' party or something.

DIANA. Classic.

HELEN. I mean, it's a tough process, figuring yourself out.

It's like… algebra.

DIANA. Hmm.

I'm sorry, what?

HELEN. Figuring out you're not straight. It's like algebra.

Beat.

DIANA. Yeah, I still don't get it.

HELEN. I just mean it's extremely hard if no one shows you how to do it. Like algebra.

DIANA. You should really get some sleep.

HELEN. Ugh, who needs sleep.

Silence.

DIANA. But I guess you're right. If you never see anyone doing it…

The thing is, I've known that I find women attractive for a really long time. There was a girl in Year 9 that I desperately, desperately… I don't even know how to describe it. I guess I just wanted to be close to her. As close as possible. And there's always been girls, here and there, that I wanted to kiss, that I fancied, I just thought…

I just thought they were all

Exceptions to the rule?

I don't know.

I never saw that feeling as… as a real part of myself.

I guess.

Does that make sense?

Beat.

Are you asleep?

HELEN. What? No. I'm awake, you want to kiss girls, I'm awake.

DIANA. You're terrible.

HELEN. Sorry.

DIANA. I was pouring my heart out.

HELEN. It's been a long day.

DIANA. And you just fall asleep on me –

HELEN. I'm sorry.

DIANA. And my innermost feelings.

HELEN. I'm pretty sure I heard most of it. You were in love with a girl in Year 9 and wow, by the way, Year 9, that's really early to know anything and –

Oh my God.

DIANA. Hmm?

HELEN. No.

DIANA. What?

HELEN. Am I – Was I your first kiss with a girl?

DIANA.…..Maybe.

HELEN. Maybe?

DIANA. Shut up.

HELEN. That was a yes or no question.

Silence.

Year 9. Damn.

Silence.

—

HELEN. This is how it ends.

I go home for my mum's birthday.

DIANA. Home is not far away.

HELEN. But it's definitely a 'gone for the whole day' sort of trip. It's just family.

My mum.

DIANA. Grandparents.

HELEN. My brother.

DIANA. And his girlfriend Mia.

HELEN. She brought a lovely, like, basket of self-care-y things for my mum.

DIANA. A basket of what now?

HELEN. You know. Shampoo, bath salts, high-end wine gums, a small fluffy towel, a tiny bottle of rosé and a lady detective novel.

DIANA. Ah.

HELEN. My brother brought some news.

DIANA. Oh?

HELEN. As soon as he says

DIANA. We have some news.

HELEN. Every fork around the table freezes in mid-air.

You can actually feel the attention in the room concentrating on him.

I can see Mia trying not to smile and failing miserably.

I think everyone can feel what my brother is going to say, even the dogs.

He says –

DIANA. We're engaged.

HELEN. And then there's just this – explosion of happiness for them.

Mia shows us the ring.

My mum gets up to hug her.

My grandpa pats my brother on the back.

I think my brother is crying a little.

My grandma is definitely crying a lot.

The whole room is full of congratulations and excitement and well-wishes and smiles and metaphorical balloons and just –

Love.

I'm so happy for them.

Everyone is so happy for them.

I am too.

So happy.

Honestly, so happy.

I'm just –

DIANA. Are you –

HELEN. So happy.

DIANA. Okay?

HELEN. Of course.

No, genuinely.

Mia is fantastic and my brother is the best person in the world and I have never wanted two people to get married as much as I have wanted these two to get married.

DIANA. But?

HELEN. As soon as my brother is done talking about the venue they're thinking of renting. As soon as Mia is done talking about the caterer they're thinking of hiring. As soon as the most urgent questions about the engagement have been answered, Mum turns to me and asks –

DIANA. What about you, darling? How's the love life?

HELEN *sighs*.

HELEN. I say

I am… not getting married.

DIANA. And your mum says –

HELEN. Nothing.

DIANA. Nothing?

HELEN. Yes, the conversation moves on. Mia starts to describe her ideal dessert menu, my brother chimes in and says that he's not going to do a stag night because people saying they need to have 'one last night of freedom' probably consider marriage a prison and should not get married. The sound of cutlery on plates starts up again, coffee is refilled, conversations overlap until –

DIANA. Until?

HELEN. I could've just let it go.

DIANA. What did you do?

HELEN. I say –

I am not getting married.

The conversation has very much moved on. Everyone looks a bit confused. My brother probably thinks I'm having a stroke or something.

So I say

I am not getting married.

But I am seeing someone.

And my grandma says exactly what I thought she would say, she says –

DIANA. Who is the lucky boy?

HELEN. And because I've been expecting it, I say, with all my confidence –

It's a girl. A woman. I mean, you know, not like a girl, she's fully grown, I mean she's – she is a she.

At first what I hear is this –

Silence. Long silence.

And then I hear something that sounds like –

DIANA *claps*.

And I think I must be going crazy because it sounds so much like clapping. It turns out that's because it is actually

DIANA *claps*.

My grandpa clapping.

DIANA. Clapping.

HELEN. Clapping. And he says –

DIANA. That's marvellous, honey.

HELEN. My grandfather thinks it's

DIANA. Marvellous, honey

HELEN. That I'm dating a girl.

He think it's

DIANA. Marvellous, honey

HELEN. That I'm dating a person of the same gender.

He is seventy years old and he thinks it is

DIANA. Marvellous, honey

HELEN. That his granddaughter is… getting some.

Nothing else that day comes close to that reaction. Nothing else ever will.

My mum wants to know details, which I mostly try to avoid because

DIANA. She knows me.

HELEN. But not

DIANA. Like that.

HELEN. My brother's reaction is just what I thought it would be, it's just –

Shrug.

Mia is super-cool about it and I think she's probably proud of herself for being so cool about it.

It's just my grandma –

DIANA. What about her?

HELEN. It's not even offensive, it's just… mildly stupid.

She says

DIANA. So you are dating a woman?

HELEN. Yes, Grandma.

DIANA. Oh.

HELEN. Yes, Grandma.

DIANA. So is it just…

HELEN. Yes, Grandma?

DIANA. Women for you?

HELEN. No, Grandma.

DIANA. Oh.

HELEN. Yes, Grandma.

DIANA. So you are going to go back to men eventually.

Pause. Silence.

HELEN. I wish I had a good reply to that.

But I just say –

I might. I might not.

DIANA. But what you wanted to say was –

HELEN. Can't you just be happy for me?

I hope that's not what I'll remember. When I look back at this. I hope that's not what I'll remember. I hope what I'll remember is this sound –

DIANA *claps*.

I hope what I'll remember is my grandpa pulling me aside before I leave and saying –

HELEN *chokes up a bit*.

Can you? [say it?]

DIANA. Sure.

HELEN. I hope what I'll remember is him saying –

DIANA. It's not important who you love. What's important is that you love someone who loves you. What's important is that you love someone who's proud to love you.

Silence.

HELEN. I hope that's what I'll remember.

—

DIANA. Just so you're aware.

HELEN. Yes?

DIANA. I had to go the hospital yesterday.

HELEN. Is this a conversation we should be having over text?

DIANA. Wait till I finish typing, would you?

He was still up when I came home yesterday and he was wondering why I was late and I panicked and said I had to go to the hospital.

HELEN. You what?

DIANA. I panicked.

I know it's stupid.

I said I banged my head at your place and we just wanted to make sure I didn't have a concussion.

HELEN. That's the funniest thing I've heard all day.

DIANA. Shut up.

HELEN. Thank you.

DIANA. So just in case it comes up tonight.

That's the story I'm going with.

HELEN. Wait.

What's tonight?

DIANA. Dinner?

With my parents and everyone?

To celebrate that my contract got extended?

HELEN. Fuck.

Sorry.

Shit.

Fuck.

DIANA. Did you forget?

HELEN. I forgot.

I'm sorry.

I've got my brother over tonight. Wedding stuff.

DIANA. It's fine.

HELEN. Sorry.

DIANA. Honestly.

HELEN. You'll be in good company though, right?

DIANA. Yeah.

I just thought it would be nice to have everyone there to celebrate.

HELEN. Ah yes.

You know what they say.

A celebration is never complete without the girl you're having an affair with.

DIANA. You don't have to joke about that.

HELEN. Sorry.

I'll make it up to you next week.

DIANA. Filthy.

HELEN. I am sorry though.

You know I'm proud of you, right?

Massively proud.

DIANA. It's fine.

I just would have liked to have my best friend there.

—

DIANA. In the library when I found a book about the gay history of Berlin.

Every time I walk by your flat, which is –

HELEN. Pretty often.

DIANA. Every time I eat anything with broccoli in it.

HELEN. I hate that stuff.

DIANA. I know.

On my way to work.

Every time someone mentions detective novels.

Whenever I read a film review.

When someone mispronounces gnocchi.

Sometimes when I masturbate.

HELEN. Only sometimes?

DIANA *looks at* HELEN. HELEN *looks at* DIANA.

DIANA. Jealous?

HELEN. Bit.

DIANA. Oh and –

When I'm hungry.

HELEN. When you're hungry?

DIANA. Correct.

What about you?

HELEN. I don't know.

DIANA. Come on, that's not fair.

HELEN. Life isn't fair.

DIANA. Oh God. Are you alright?

HELEN. I don't know.

Beat.

I guess it would be easier to list the times when I don't think of you.

—

HELEN. Do you have everything?

DIANA. I think so.

I mean, if not –

HELEN. I'll just bring it tomorrow.

DIANA. Right, just bring it tomorrow.

Okay then.

HELEN. Wait, sorry, just, before you go.

DIANA. Yeah?

HELEN. Do you think anyone suspects anything?

About us?

I mean, someone must suspect something.

DIANA. I don't think so.

Why?

HELEN. No reason.

I'm just worried, I guess.

DIANA. Don't be.

We are good at this.

HELEN. Really good.

You're right.

Anyway, have you got your phone?

DIANA. Got it.

Ready to go.

HELEN. Great.

DIANA. Actually... Have I told you this?

HELEN. What?

DIANA. Do you remember when we went to the cinema last month? With Maeve and everyone?

HELEN. Yeah.

DIANA. Big group. Eight, ten, people?

HELEN. And?

DIANA. And we were standing around in the foyer and Maeve was handing out the tickets but she did it in this weird way, sort of cutting back and forth across the circle?

HELEN. Right.

DIANA. Anyway, I was standing next to you and I looked over at your ticket. To check your seat number. To see if it was next to mine. Can't have taken more than a second. But I think Maeve saw. And she looked at me sort of... knowingly.

HELEN. How do you look at someone knowingly?

DIANA. I don't know. She just smiled at me in a weird way, it was somewhere between 'that's sweet' and 'that's pathetic'.

HELEN. So do you think she knew?

DIANA. No.

Maybe.

I don't think so, I mean –

HELEN. We're really good at this.

DIANA. Yeah, really good.

HELEN. At hiding.

Silence.

I just think it's unlikely.

That no one suspects anything.

I mean

We held hands throughout that whole film.

DIANA. Yeah, but.

I don't think anyone is suspicious.

Maybe if I start kissing you in front of everyone.

But even then.

HELEN. Yeah.

Silence.

Have you got your keys?

DIANA. Yes.

Wait.

No.

I'll get them.

HELEN. Okay.

Silence.

But I guess it is, isn't it?

DIANA. What?

HELEN. Somewhere between sweet and pathetic.

—

HELEN. This is how it ends.

I go to this conference for work one weekend. Boring people, great canapés.

DIANA. This is in –

HELEN. November, I think?

DIANA. Yeah.

HELEN. I come home, I walk through the door and my first
thought is

DIANA. Fuck, it's cold.

HELEN. That's my first thought.

And my flat isn't

DIANA. Warm

HELEN. At the best of times.

It's not

DIANA. Tropical.

HELEN. It's not the kind of flat where you would want to walk
around naked.

Even if you really liked walking around naked.

You wouldn't want to do it in my flat.

DIANA. Learned that the hard way.

HELEN. Yeah, sorry.

When I get home, it's really cold, even for my flat. I check
the radiators and they've all gone completely cold, like
they're switched off. And it's Sunday evening and I try to
ring my landlord about five times but of course he doesn't
pick up his phone because why would he.

And at this point, I don't really know what to do and I'm
tired and hungry, so I do the only reasonable thing and –

DIANA. Sit around and do nothing.

HELEN. After about ten minutes of very productive sitting
around doing nothing, I text you.

I say –

DIANA. I think the heating is broken.

HELEN. And then I sit around some more.

DIANA. Can I ask –

HELEN. Yeah?

DIANA. Why didn't you just call?

HELEN. It's Sunday evening.

Beat.

DIANA. Oh yeah.

Right.

HELEN. Anyway, I sit around a bit longer.

I text you again.

I say –

DIANA. I'm freezing.

HELEN. Because I am.

And I'm just thinking about how many sweaters I can wear on top of each other, when you text back, you say –

DIANA. Oh my God, come over here.

HELEN. You say –

DIANA. You can sleep here.

HELEN. You say –

DIANA. I don't want you to be cold.

HELEN. I'm basically still packed from the conference, so all I have to do is throw some fresh clothes into my backpack. I'm already halfway through the door again when I think the silliest thing that's crossed my mind in a long time, I think –

DIANA *breathes in as if to start talking but* HELEN *speaks before* DIANA *can.*

And I blame the freezing cold for this entirely, I think –

DIANA *takes another breath.*

I mean, really, keep in mind, this is the product of a frozen brain, I think –

DIANA *takes another breath, waits for* HELEN *to interrupt her. She doesn't.*

No, go on, I'm done.

I think –

DIANA. Maybe I should put on sexier underwear.

HELEN. Maybe I should put on sexier underwear.

I think, maybe I should put on sexier underwear.

I'm standing in the hallway.

I've already got my backpack on.

I'm ready to go.

…

…

…

I put on sexier underwear.

Purple.

The lacy kind.

A couple of minutes later, I'm at your doorstep and your boyfriend opens the door and gives me a hug.

DIANA. He gives you a hug.

HELEN. And he says –

DIANA. Poor you, you must be freezing, come in.

HELEN. Poor me.

DIANA. Poor you.

HELEN. It's Sunday, you've made dinner together.

He says –

DIANA. You're crashing our date night.

HELEN. It's Sunday.

You've made dinner together.

DIANA. Really nice dinner.

HELEN. Delicious.

DIANA. Linguine with ricotta, shallots and thyme.

It's good.

HELEN. So good.

DIANA. So good.

HELEN. So good, it actually makes me a bit angry.

DIANA. Why would that make you / angry?

HELEN. We sit at your kitchen table, the three of us and it should be awkward.

DIANA. It's not awkward.

HELEN. But it should be awkward.

DIANA. Do you want it to be awkward?

HELEN. You pile up pasta on my plate.

That's enough.

DIANA. Bit more.

HELEN. Okay.

Your boyfriend pours me a glass of wine.

DIANA. Good wine.

HELEN. Great wine.

He does that thing posh people do with wine, you know –

She mimes 'letting the wine breathe'.

When you have your first sip of wine, you both go –

HELEN *and* DIANA. Aaaaah.

HELEN. I'm sitting across from you.

And I get this idea.

So I slouch in my chair slightly, like this.

HELEN *mimes what she's doing.*

And I stretch my leg a bit more.

Bit more.

And then I hear –

DIANA. Is that your foot?

HELEN. Says your boyfriend.

Your boyfriend says –

DIANA. Is that your foot?

And you say

HELEN. Sorry.

Just

Stretching.

Sorry.

Won't happen again.

And he says –

DIANA. It's alright.

HELEN. It's alright.

He starts recommending films to me over dinner.

DIANA. Have you seen *Rashomon*?

HELEN. Yes I have.

DIANA. Have you seen *Last Year at Marienbad*?

HELEN. Yes I have.

DIANA. Have you seen *À Bout de Souffle*?

HELEN. He says –

DIANA. *À Bout de Souffle*.

HELEN. He doesn't say *Breathless*, he says –

DIANA. *À Bout de Souffle*.

HELEN *giggles*.

Is that funny?

HELEN *shrugs*.

HELEN. A bit.

You don't think so?

DIANA. That's just what it's called, isn't it?

HELEN. Yeah, it's just –

DIANA. What?

HELEN. Nothing

Just

Beat.

(*Basically just vowels*.) *À Bout de Souffle*.

Doesn't matter, yes, I have seen *À Bout de Souffle*, mind you, I have a master's degree in film studies.

DIANA. He says he'll come up with a recommendation for you.

HELEN. Something I haven't seen.

While he washes up, you say –

DIANA. Follow me.

HELEN. And I do.

I follow you into your bedroom.

And it's weird because –

I don't think I've ever been in your bedroom.

It's just not where we go

When I'm here.

It's a proper adult's bedroom. There are framed prints on the wall, a stack of books on your bedside table. I didn't know your boyfriend had reading glasses. And the bed looks –

Soft. Solid. Comfortable.

Nice mattress. Two pillows. Really fluffy pillows.

I get this random, sudden urge to grab you and tackle you onto the bed and pull you on top of me. I know exactly what kind of sound you would make if I did that. I know exactly how your body would feel on top of mine.

But I've never –

I've never been in your bed.

DIANA. There you go.

HELEN. You say –

DIANA. There you go.

HELEN. You hand me a towel from your wardrobe.

You leave the bedroom.

I follow you into the living room.

You show me the sofa, you say –

DIANA. Your bed for tonight.

And then you say

HELEN. Thank you.

DIANA. But then you say –

HELEN. It's not really a bed though, is it?

DIANA. What do you mean?

HELEN. Well, it's a sofa.

DIANA *looks at* HELEN, *confused*.

I mean, thank you, obviously, it's lovely, the blanket is lovely and you've done your best to make it resemble a bed but –

It's still a sofa.

It's obviously

Still a sofa.

So, really, you should have said

Your sofa for tonight.

Not

Your bed for tonight.

Don't you think?

You say

DIANA. Are you okay?

And you –

HELEN *exhales*.

HELEN. Sorry.

Long day.

And then you put your arms around me, one hand here

The back of HELEN*'s right shoulder.*

One hand here.

Her lower back.

Your lips here.

The left side of her neck.

And then you pull back and you look at me.

DIANA. And you look at me.

HELEN. Your hands are still where they've been a thousand
times by now.

And then I hear –

DIANA. *In the Mood for Love?*

HELEN. Your boyfriend says –

DIANA. Have you seen *In the Mood for Love?*

Silence.

HELEN. My instinct is to jump away from you.

DIANA. My instinct is not to.

HELEN. Clearly, because you keep holding me in your arms –

DIANA. Why would I jump away from you?

HELEN. You even give him a little smile while you keep
holding me in your arms.

Silence. If there was physical contact, HELEN *breaks it.*
DIANA *stands still, frozen in an incomplete hug.*

I mean, he must have –

He must've seen that.

Surely.

DIANA. We were just hugging. We hug all the time.

HELEN. You were looking at me.

DIANA. I know.

HELEN. I mean, you were looking at me.

If I was –

Never mind.

DIANA. If you were what?

HELEN. Forget it.

DIANA. What were you going to say?

Beat.

HELEN. If I was a guy, he'd be punching me in the face right now.

Think about it.

DIANA. He wouldn't.

HELEN. I think he would.

DIANA. He doesn't do punching.

HELEN. I think he'd make an exception.

DIANA. Do you want to be punched in the face?

HELEN. Maybe!

DIANA. Maybe?

HELEN. This is stupid.

HELEN *returns to* DIANA*'s embrace.*

Where were we?

Oh yes.

I have seen *In the Mood for Love.*

He says –

DIANA. I can't win with you, you've seen everything.

HELEN. And I say –

Don't let it bother you, you've seen an awful lot.

He says

DIANA. Goodnight.

HELEN. You say

DIANA. Goodnight.

HELEN. I say –

DIANA. Good/night

HELEN. Goodnight.

> And then you two are off to bed.
>
> And I lie down on the sofa.
>
> And I had almost forgotten the most ridiculous, stupid, idiotic part of this.
>
> But my brain doesn't work like that.
>
> So here's the most ridiculous, stupid, idiotic part of this.
>
> I'm wearing sexy underwear.

—

DIANA. Did they fix your radiators?

> My sofa is yours if you need it.
>
> Your landlord is paying for this, right?
>
> Are you okay?
>
> Do you want to come over for dinner?

HELEN. I don't think we should be having this conversation over text.

> *Silence.*

—

HELEN. This is how it ends.

> I'm at the pub with some of my colleagues one Friday and I don't know if it's because it's the end of the week or because it'll be Christmas soon or maybe we're just all feeling a bit morbid but one of my colleagues asks –

DIANA. If you only had one day left to live, what would you do?

HELEN. For a minute, everyone goes –

> *Huffing and puffing, drinking.*
>
> Then Karen next to me goes –

DIANA. Organise a huge dinner for all my friends and family.

HELEN. Everyone goes –

HELEN *and* DIANA. Awwww.

HELEN. Except for the guy who asked the question, who says –

DIANA. That's stupid.

HELEN. Karen goes –

DIANA. Excuse me?

HELEN. And he goes –

DIANA. I mean, sure, you're around people you love and all that crap, but think about it. You'd spend half the day shopping for groceries and cooking. Half the day. Of your last day on earth. You want to do something that you really enjoy, on your last day on earth.

HELEN. So Karen asks him –

DIANA. Go on then, what would you do?

HELEN. And he says –

DIANA. Eat lots of cheeseburgers, have lots of sex.

HELEN. And Karen asks –

DIANA. Is that before or after the cheeseburgers?

HELEN. And he says –

DIANA. Good question, Karen. That's during.

HELEN. And then Karen turns towards me and asks

DIANA. What about you?

If you only had one day left to live –

What would you do?

—

DIANA. Have you seen my bra anywhere?

HELEN. Is it under your sweater?

DIANA. No.

HELEN. Under my sweater?

DIANA. No. How does this happen every time?

HELEN. Can I ask you a weird question?

DIANA. Will it help me find my bra?

HELEN. No.

DIANA. Then no.

HELEN. If you only had one day left to live –

DIANA. Yes?

HELEN. I mean, just one day, a single day –

DIANA. Yes?

HELEN. Would you sleep with him or with me?

DIANA. What?

HELEN. Who would you sleep with? Him or me?

Beat.

DIANA. I don't know.

HELEN. Take your time.

Silence.

DIANA. No, I genuinely don't know.

HELEN. If you had to choose.

DIANA. Do I have to?

HELEN. No, of course not.

Beat.

But say you had to.

DIANA. Can't I just sleep with both of you?

HELEN. Well –

DIANA. I mean, if it's a whole day, I could totally sleep with both of you –

HELEN. Yeah but –

DIANA. Although I suppose I'd have to do other stuff as well, right? Go see my family. God, no, that would take ages, they

would have to come to me. I think. I'd like to go to the
cinema one last time, actually. But what if they're not
showing anything I want to see? I guess I could / ask them to
do a special screening.

HELEN. Would you tell him?

Silence.

DIANA. I'll check under the sofa.

HELEN. Do you think you would tell him?

DIANA. It must be here somewhere.

HELEN. Did you hear what I said?

DIANA. About us? Would I tell him about us?

Silence.

I don't think I would.

Silence.

Okay?

HELEN. Okay.

Silence.

But if you only had one day –

DIANA. Why do you want me dead so badly?

Beat.

HELEN. I don't –

I'm not –

DIANA. Are you saying you want me to tell him?

HELEN. Of course not, I'm just saying. Theoretically.

DIANA. Theoretically, I should tell him?

HELEN. Forget it. Did you check the bathroom?

DIANA. Why would it be in the bathroom?

Silence.

Would you?

HELEN. Check the bathroom?

DIANA. Would you tell him?

HELEN. Of course not.

DIANA. You wouldn't?

HELEN. Wait, am I dying or are you dying?

DIANA. I'm dying.

HELEN. No, I wouldn't.

DIANA. Why not?

HELEN. I wouldn't.

>   It's not my…

>   It's not my confession to make.

DIANA. Confession?

HELEN. Yeah.

DIANA. Like in church?

HELEN. No, confession, as in –

DIANA. He's not my priest, he's my boyfriend.

HELEN. I just meant a normal confession.

DIANA. Like some kind of authority figure.

HELEN. A normal non-Catholic confession.

DIANA. It's just –

>   Confession makes it sound like I've done something wrong.

HELEN. And you haven't.

DIANA. We haven't.

HELEN. No.

>   *Beat.*

DIANA. Well, it's official.

>   There's a black hole in your bedroom and it's eaten my bra.

>   And I'm gonna miss my train home.

HELEN *produces the bra.*

HELEN. Merry Christmas.

—

DIANA. Here are some things that I almost text you from the train but then delete.

Are you okay?

I hope you know that this is not just a casual thing for me.

Do you want me to tell him?

Do you want this to end?

I don't want to be a cliché.

Is this enough for you?

Am I enough for you?

I want this to be something good. For both of us.

—

HELEN. This is how it ends.

I go home over Christmas and it's all –

DIANA. Cookies and hugs and slightly scratchy jumpers.

HELEN. I'm decorating the Christmas tree with my mum. She has a thing for ornaments that look like famous landmarks, so that's what we're using. We're just decorating away when she asks –

DIANA. Do you know what book I'm reading at the moment?

HELEN. And I bite back a snarky response and say –

What book are you reading, Mum?

I'm expecting something with a murder in a nice seaside town and a light-hearted love story because that's what it usually is.

But Mum says –

DIANA. I'm reading this book about the lives of lesbians in the 1970s.

HELEN. She says lesbians very carefully, like she's just learnt the word.

DIANA. Lesbians.

HELEN. And I almost drop the Eiffel Tower ornament I was holding.

Where –

Where did you get a book about the lives of lesbians in the 1970s, Mum?

DIANA. This new bookshop in town has an LGBT section –

HELEN. She says LGBT very carefully, like she just learnt the alphabet.

DIANA. LGBT.

HELEN. My face is all question marks.

DIANA. That's where I found the book.

It's a very interesting read.

HELEN. My mum is really overcompensating on the whole 'having a queer daughter' front.

It makes me want to buy her ten more landmark ornaments.

DIANA. It's a very interesting read.

HELEN. Is it?

DIANA. Yes. But very tough, too.

I mean, it's just terrible how much your people had to hide back then.

HELEN. I don't want to ruin the moment but I say it anyway, I say –

Mum, I'm bisexual, not a lesbian.

And she says –

DIANA. I know that. But they're still your people, aren't they?

HELEN. And I say –

Yes, of course they are.

DIANA. They didn't have much on bisexuality in the LGBT section, darling.

I'll show you next time we're in town.

HELEN. Okay.

DIANA. I'm just glad –

HELEN. She says it carefully, like she learnt it by heart.

DIANA. I'm just glad you have it easier.

—

HELEN. Here are some things that I almost text you but then delete over the next few days.

Look, I know this was never meant to be more than a casual thing.

My mum bought a book about lesbians in the seventies.

I really, really, really, really, really miss you.

There's this straight couple in the seats behind me on the train and they keep kissing and I hate them.

I know I'm being stupid.

If your boyfriend was a dick, this would be so much easier.

DIANA. Maybe we should have had these conversations.

HELEN. But not over text.

—

DIANA. This is how it ends.

I come back from Christmas at my parents' house five books and three pounds heavier.

HELEN. It suits you.

DIANA. The pounds?

HELEN. And the books.

DIANA. I come back from Christmas at my parents' house on the 31st of December, around noon.

Like every year, some of our friends are throwing a party –

HELEN. At the house they share, so the party can spread all over the house.

DIANA. Everyone's invited, friends, friends of friends –

HELEN. Plus partners.

DIANA. Plus partners, so it's packed.

HELEN. Beyond packed.

DIANA. It's always great.

HELEN. It is, it's the best.

DIANA. As soon as I get home, I text you, I ask when you're leaving for the party and you text back

HELEN. I'm not going.

Beat.

DIANA. Wait, you're –

HELEN. Not going.

You text back

DIANA. Are you sick?

HELEN. Because that's the only explanation you can think of for me not going, you think I'm –

DIANA. Sick.

But you say

HELEN. No, I'm fine.

I mean, I'm healthy.

Whatever.

I just don't want to go.

You say –

DIANA. But what are going to do at midnight?

And you say

HELEN. I don't know.

DIANA. I don't understand. Because everyone's there, friends, friends of friends.

HELEN. Plus partners.

DIANA. Plus –

Oh.

Plus –

HELEN. Yeah.

DIANA. I text you again, I say –

He's not coming.

By the way.

And you say –

HELEN *types, deletes, types, deletes.*

HELEN. Really?

You say

DIANA. Yeah.

You say

HELEN. Pick me up around seven?

—

HELEN. Here are some of the things that happen that night.

DIANA. Someone throws up in the kitchen sink.

HELEN. Two of our friends have an argument –

DIANA. An actual argument

HELEN. About the best type of hummus.

DIANA. Someone tinkers with the playlist

HELEN. Everything goes eerily quiet.

DIANA. Until someone starts singing 'Hit Me Baby One More Time'

HELEN. And a whole choir of people joins in.

DIANA. Two of our friends break up.

HELEN. Not the two who fought about hummus.

DIANA. Two others.

HELEN. Two others.

DIANA. The two with the hummus –

HELEN. Actually make out in the bathroom.

DIANA. There is lots of dancing

HELEN. Lots of touching

DIANA. Lots of cigarettes

HELEN. Lots of music

DIANA. Lots of anticipation

HELEN. For the year to be over

DIANA. For the year to begin

HELEN. And we –

DIANA. We dance too closely

HELEN. We sing too loudly

DIANA. We laugh too much

HELEN. We care too little

DIANA. We don't care at all.

HELEN. And when the countdown approaches

DIANA. When the wait is nearly over

HELEN. We all go outside

DIANA. It's freezing

HELEN. It's so cold

DIANA. We go outside with sparkling wine

HELEN. We go outside with sparklers

DIANA. We go outside in our sparkling outfits.

HELEN. Everyone is standing around

DIANA. Sweat freezing on their skin

HELEN. And then the countdown starts –

DIANA. Ten

HELEN. Everyone is shouting

DIANA. Nine

HELEN. We're surrounded by our friends

DIANA. Eight

HELEN. Everyone can see us

DIANA. Seven

HELEN. No one is watching us

DIANA. Six

HELEN. My hand is in your hand

DIANA. Five

HELEN. And your face is next to mine

DIANA. Four

HELEN. Soon there will be cheering

DIANA. Three

HELEN. Fireworks and people shouting

DIANA. Two

HELEN. But I don't think I will notice

DIANA. One

HELEN. Anything but you.

A kiss. Fireworks. Sparklers. 'Auld Lang Syne'. Noise, but far off, like HELEN *and* DIANA *are in a bubble.*

—

HELEN. It ends three hours later.

The party is still going but I can feel that everyone who is still here is having slightly more fun than me.

DIANA. The playlist is starting to become a bit dodgy.

HELEN. My make-up is starting to self-destruct.

DIANA. People have mostly stopped dancing, except for a brave few.

HELEN. We've escaped to the kitchen.

DIANA. It's that point of the night where you either go home immediately

HELEN. Or stick around for three more hours.

DIANA. And we decide

HELEN. To go home.

DIANA (*at the same time*). To stick around.

They smile.

Let's go home.

HELEN. Are you sure?

DIANA. I am.

HELEN. We decide to go home.

DIANA. We decide to walk.

HELEN. Because we need some air that no one danced in.

DIANA. Because we're ready to leave but not ready for the night to end.

HELEN. Technically, it's already morning.

DIANA. But it still feels like last night.

HELEN. I grab a half-empty bottle of wine.

DIANA. For the journey.

HELEN. And off we go.

DIANA. It ends ten minutes later.

When we have said goodbye to everyone and we're walking down the street and you look at me like this.

HELEN *still looks straight ahead.*

HELEN. And you look at me like that.

DIANA *still looks straight ahead.*

And I say –

DIANA *puts her finger on* HELEN's *lips.*

DIANA. Not yet, okay?

HELEN. Okay.

>*They stay together in silence, not doing anything in
>particular, just the calm before the storm.*
>
>*This should take a while.*
>
>*Then* HELEN *looks at* DIANA.
>
>DIANA *nods.*

DIANA. And you say –

HELEN. I think this is it.

>And you say

DIANA. Yeah.

>Yeah, I think it is.

HELEN. And then you say nothing until you say –

DIANA. I don't want to lose you.

>And you say –

HELEN. You won't.

>You don't say anything.
>
>So I say it again.
>
>You won't.
>
>*Silence.*
>
>It ends five minutes later.

DIANA. When you say –

HELEN. We could just fuck off.

>Right now.
>
>To Berlin or –
>
>Somewhere.
>
>We could leave.
>
>Right now.
>
>*Silence.*
>
>It ends when I laugh.

DIANA. It ends when I laugh.

HELEN. It ends when you say –

DIANA. I don't think there are any three a.m. flights to Berlin.

HELEN. Have you checked?

DIANA. Yeah.

It ends when you say –

HELEN. No.

I suppose there aren't.

It ends when we arrive at my doorstep.

DIANA. It ends when you say

HELEN. Well.

Although I'm not.

I'm not well.

At all.

It ends when you take my hand and put my fingers to your lips.

DIANA. Like an overeager guy at the end of a date.

HELEN. Like a knight in a fairy tale.

DIANA. It ends when you kiss me.

HELEN. It ends when you stop kissing me.

DIANA. I want to say it's different than all our other kisses.

HELEN. But it's not.

DIANA. No it's not.

HELEN. That's when it ends.

Silence.

I'll see you on Sunday, right?

DIANA. At the?

HELEN. The brunch thing?

DIANA. Brunch thing, yeah. I'll be there.

HELEN. Good. Me too.

DIANA. Good.

Silence.

I don't know what else to say.

HELEN. Me neither.

DIANA *shrugs.*

HELEN *shrugs.*

Silence.

HELEN *does that thing where she waves but also stretches her arm out for* DIANA.

DIANA *does the same thing.*

Their fingers are almost touching.

And that's where it ends.

I FUCKED YOU IN MY SPACESHIP

Louis Emmitt-Stern

LOUIS EMMITT-STERN

Louis Emmitt-Stern is an award-winning writer and director from Gibraltar, now based in London. His debut full-length play, *Slippery*, won Soho Theatre's Tony Craze Award 2021. His work has been performed at Soho Theatre, Watford Palace Theatre, Southwark Playhouse, The Pleasance Theatre, Islington, Ivy Arts Centre, and supported by Farnham Maltings.

Louis trained at Guildford School of Acting, and the Royal Central School of Speech and Drama. He is an alumnus of the Gibraltar Academy of Music and Performing Arts, Soho Theatre Writers Lab, Soho Writers Alumni Group, National Theatre Young Playwrights Programme, and Young Lyric Directors Course at Lyric Hammersmith.

Louis was a finalist for a HM Government of Gibraltar Cultural Award for his production of Duncan Macmillan's *Lungs*, and for his work with young people in the arts and education. He teaches acting and playwriting both in the UK and Gibraltar.

I Fucked You in My Spaceship was first performed at VAULT
Festival, London, on 7 February 2023, with the following cast:

LEO	Jonas Moore
DAN	Max Hyner
AL	Felix Kai
ANNA	Rebecca Banatvala
EMILY	Lucy Spreckley
ROBERT	Lewis Shepherd

Director	Joseph Winer
Lighting Designer	Laura Howard
Sound Designer	Bella Kear
Movement Director	Patrice Bowler
Stage Manager	Caelan Oram
Casting Associates	Megha Dhingra
	Clarice Montero

Characters

LEO
DAN, *his boyfriend*
AL, *a stranger*
ANNA
EMILY, *her girlfriend*
ROBERT, *a student*

Characters can be any race.

Setting

Leo, Dan, and Al's story takes place in Leo and Dan's apartment, and a nearby café.

Anna, Emily, and Robert's story takes place in Anna and Emily's apartment.

Both stories take place in the same universe, orbiting the same sun, and in doing so, orbit one another.

Note on Text

This play is written to be performed on a bare stage. There should be no scenery, no mime, no props, and no furniture unless explicitly stated.

Blackouts between scenes should be avoided.

(/) indicates the point of interruption in overlapping dialogue.

(…) indicates trailing off.

(–) indicates interruption. Within speech it indicates a break in syntax.

(,) on a separate line indicates deliberate silence from pressure, expectation or desire to speak.

Lines in [square brackets] are unspoken, indicating an unfinished thought.

Punctuation is used freely and artistically to suggest delivery, not to conform to grammatical rules.

Prologue

Space. The Final Frontier.

The main theme from 2001: A Space Odyssey *(1968) plays.*

Heavy breathing begins to overlap. Like an astronaut in a space helmet. It gets louder and more sexual.

The music is about to reach its crescendo when…

Everything stops.

One

LEO *and* DAN.

LEO	No sorry not – Not 'STOP!' Sorry just a minute sorry
DAN	Am I doing something / wrong?
LEO	No you're
DAN	If there's something I'm not getting…
LEO	Doing great, baby
DAN	Do you want some water?
LEO	Doing great mostly
DAN	Might get some water. Mostly?
LEO	You're trying, *really* trying, and that's… Thank you.
DAN	I am.
LEO	Yes yes baby, I know, I know you are And that's beautiful. That's enough.
DAN	It's not working?
LEO	No it's good it's Maybe the voice
DAN	The voice?
LEO	Not quite the same.
DAN	I'm sweating Going to get / some water.

LEO   It's a little more gentle, really
            If you watch the YouTube clips, the voice is
            more gentle

DAN   I was being gentle.

LEO   Okay okay yes sure.
            But,
            No. Not really.
            You were going for more of a 'husky' thing

DAN   I don't think so

LEO   A little too husky
            And I know that's part of it

DAN   That's not really…

LEO   When you're in the moment
            and you're inside me
            and saying my name
            and it's heavy breathing
            it's husky it's

DAN   Hard to breathe in the costume

LEO   But if you listen to the clip it's much more gentle
            And I understand why you'd think that
            because,
            You know,
            There's a prejudice…
            no not prejudice,
            a sort of…
            stereotype.
            Yes.
            Isn't there.

DAN   Is there?

LEO   That's husky – not husky not… just all
            'GRAHHHH' and like
            aggressive
            and
            violent
            and

DAN   I'm not being violent.

LEO   No no,
           No.
           Of course you're not
           But to some extent you've got this predetermined
           idea that they're violent
           and that's not your fault.
           Its the media, really,
           But it's about recognising that it's only
           a stereotype
           And most aliens
           Once you get past that
           Are actually quite gentle and peaceful
           And I think if you rewatch the YouTube clip
           you'll get that

           Because I want to believe you.
           Like fuck me, you know.
           Like you've abducted me and you're fucking me
           in your spaceship
           And that's hot.
           And I'm there, I'm almost there
           And I think if the voice was a little more gentle
           It'd be like fireworks
           Don't you think?

DAN   …

LEO   ?

DAN   ,

           Can we try it without the costume?

LEO   Don't you think if –

           ,

           What?

DAN   I'll do the voice

LEO   You don't want to wear the costume?

DAN   It's a million degrees

LEO	It's the most important bit
DAN	Can't you imagine it?
LEO	Imagine you wearing the costume?
DAN	Sure
LEO	But that's the point of the costume. So I can imagine you / as the alien
DAN	Yes, I know the point of the costume,
LEO	Otherwise I'm imagining you wearing the costume imagining you as the alien. And that's too many steps
DAN	I'll wear it.
LEO	Well, no…
DAN	Sorry?
LEO	You have to *want* to wear it Otherwise it's not sexy it's not
DAN	It's *your* fantasy
LEO	No of course, but If you don't want it, I mean, to some extent, Well, it's a bit fucking weird, isn't it?
DAN	I do I do
LEO	You're just a guy in an alien costume.
DAN	I'm putting it on
LEO	No actually Because it's not just the costume It's the voice And a bunch of other things and
DAN	What other things? A *bunch*?
LEO	Let's have, you know, some normal sex,

DAN   I can do it

LEO   Let me finish,
We can try this again and you can be 'you'
Because you're very good at that,
And then maybe…
…we don't have to…
…But if you didn't want to play the alien

DAN   I can

LEO   Yes I know baby of course you can but
If you didn't *want* to
We can get someone else to be the alien
Someone we know
Or don't know
That's entirely up to us really.
Someone with a gentle voice
And they can do that,
And they can wear the costume.

DAN   Get someone else involved?

LEO   For the alien stuff.

DAN   I don't know if I want to do that.

LEO   Okay, that's okay, that's

DAN   No. I don't think… no.

           ,

Who do you have in mind?

LEO   That's something we'd / talk –

DAN   No one from the office.

LEO   ,

If you don't want that, okay.

DAN   You don't think it would be awkward?

LEO   If you think it would be awkward, I can
understand that.

DAN   You've got someone in mind. From the office.

LEO   I didn't say that.

DAN   You do. You fucking do.

LEO   No, of course not

           But

           ,

           Well,

           I mean,

           We know Ryan's into that stuff.

DAN   Ryan from HR, Ryan?

LEO   He posted those photos
           The ones from Comic Con
           On Instagram.

           ,

           And his voice

DAN   Nothing like the clip.

LEO   No, sure, but
           Potentially.
           It's got potential.

DAN   ,

           What would I do? If I'm not the alien.

LEO   What would you like?

DAN   I'll think about it.

LEO   Of course.

           ,

           And if you didn't want to be involved

           ,

           You wouldn't have to be there. If you didn't
           want to.

           ,

           I'll send Ryan the clip, see what he thinks.

Two

ANNA *and* EMILY.

ANNA   It's just a bit of a nightmare.

EMILY   Do you think?

ANNA   Nightmare to spell, really.

EMILY   I don't know.

ANNA   I'm dyslexic / basically.

EMILY   No you're not.

ANNA   Want to be able to spell my kid's name

EMILY   Not that difficult.

ANNA   Don't want people to struggle
            To spell it.

EMILY   Fuck those people.

ANNA   No. Of course.
            Fuck those people. Of course.
            But like, what about her?
            Always getting your name mis-spelt.
            At school. On autographs.
            It's a bit of a faff.

EMILY   Niamh (?)

ANNA   Don't want to do that to our child.

EMILY   I've crossed it out.

ANNA   I think that's best.

EMILY   I've got Bernadette on the 'maybe' list.

ANNA   Bernadette?

EMILY   It's vintage.

ANNA   It's fucking catholic that's what it is.

EMILY   It's on the maybe list.

ANNA   I'm not carrying a Bernadette

I'm not getting itchy skin and bleeding gums and
swollen ankles for a Bernadette.

EMILY   Crossing out Bernadette.

ANNA   'Is that your daughter?
'Oh lovely
'What's her name again?
'Bernadette?'

EMILY   At least if it's a boy /

ANNA   Could you imagine that? /

EMILY   If it's a boy at least we've settled on that.

ANNA   Right.

EMILY   We're decided.

ANNA   That's a big word.

EMILY   Thought we'd

ANNA   I'm very keen on it.
Keen, I think is the word.
Keen.

EMILY   What's wrong with it?

ANNA   Nothing's wrong with it.

EMILY   We like it. We like Eddie.

ANNA   (*To herself*.) 'Eddie'

EMILY   We love Eddie

ANNA   Not sure if it's really got
Much

          ,

          Sex appeal.

EMILY   Eddie Izzard, Eddie Murphy
Eddie Redmayne,

ANNA   Yes
Yes of course

EMILY	More sex appeal than Eddie fucking Redmayne?
ANNA	I get that. I do, but
EMILY	Edward Cullen.
ANNA	Don't think that's… He's a character. Characters don't count.
EMILY	Ed Norton, Eddie Cibrian
ANNA	Ed Sheeran.
EMILY	, Oh.
	,
ANNA	Exactly.
EMILY	Oh no.
ANNA	Yeah.
EMILY	We can't do that.
ANNA	That's what I thought.
EMILY	Crossing out Ed.
ANNA	Do you think maybe…
EMILY	I've crossed it out.
ANNA	Do you think maybe we're not ready?
EMILY	, No. I don't think that. Why? Do *you* think that?
ANNA	I don't know.
EMILY	I think, yes, we're ready. We both said.
ANNA	If we can't decide on a name

EMILY   Don't start this.

ANNA   I'm not.

EMILY   Don't get all...
Indecisive-y now.

It's not a real feeling.
You know this.
Always do this when you're scared.

ANNA   I've had this idea
In my head
Ever since I was little
I carried a pillow under my top and walked
around the living room

And wrapped up my teddy-unicorn in blankets
Making her little bottles of milk

Had this idea in my head for I don't know how
long

Scared of ruining that.

EMILY   We're just making a list.
That's all we're doing.

ANNA   Yes.

EMILY   Look.
A list.
That's all it is.
A piece of paper.

We don't have to make any decisions.

ANNA   I know.

EMILY   Maybe
And we'll look at their face
Into their little eyes
And we'll know.

ANNA   Do you think?

EMILY   People say that.
They say

We just saw him or her or them and
We knew.

ANNA   What if I don't know?
         What if I look down at my baby I don't know
         who they are.
         Just some... entity
         Alien to me
         Staring back.
         A nothing.

         Or worse,
         Look down and all I see is Ed Sheeran.

EMILY   I think you're overthinking this.

ANNA   Written across his forehead in big black letters.
         I don't know if I'm ready for that.

EMILY   ,

         What do you want to do?

ANNA   I don't know.

         Let's put it all under the maybe list
         And come back to it.

         Just keep it there
         Baby
         As a 'maybe'
         Until we're sure.

Three

LEO *and* DAN.

DAN   He's got a rabbit calendar.

          On his desk.

          One of those calendars with rabbits.
          With a different rabbit every month.

          And you flip it over and 'oh look, it's a white
          rabbit for April'.
          Isn't that really really really lovely.

LEO   ,

          Right.

DAN   Rabbits.

LEO   Okay.

DAN   I'm not saying don't ask.
          That's not what I'm saying.

LEO   I quite like the calendar.

DAN   By all means ask away.

LEO   Quite cute.

DAN   It's a lot to digest.

LEO   Is it?

DAN   For Ryan.

          It's quite a lot to put onto him.
          Quite a big sort of
          Gesture
          I suppose

LEO   Well

DAN   Because we've got to go to work.
          Have you thought about that?

          If he says no
          We've got to go to work with him
          And he'll

We'll all have this
Thing
This gesture that's been made
Especially
If he says no

Or if he says yes.

What if he says yes?

He says yes
And he comes over.
And then we go to work

Every day

And chat through the sales reports
Like absolutely / nothing's…

LEO   Okay

DAN   Do you see what I'm / saying?

LEO   I think so.

DAN   It's worth thinking about

LEO   Absolutely
I hear you, baby.

DAN   Thank you.

LEO   And I guess
I'm not really thinking about these things
I'm not really worried because
I didn't really think he would be
You know
That he'd be awkward about it.

DAN   No.

LEO   He's very professional.

DAN   No, of course.

LEO   I wasn't just going to come out with it.
I wasn't just going to say:
Hello Ryan.
I hope you're well.

Little opportunity for you
Would you like to come round sometime this
week and pretend to be an alien?

DAN   No / no I know.

LEO   Is Wednesday any good?
Wednesday or Thursday works well for us. Let me
know.
My very best wishes, Leo.

DAN   Of course not.

LEO   Just going to feel him out.
At first.
Just feel
See if I get a…
You know
A vibe.

DAN   Do we know him well enough?
Like that?
A *vibe*?
We don't really know him.

LEO   I know him.

DAN   Not really.

LEO   If you don't want to do this

DAN   I do.

LEO   Hey hey
I don't want you to feel pressured

DAN   I don't.
No.
I want to.

LEO   Okay.

DAN   Been having a look.
As an idea.
This website.

LEO   Oh?

DAN   You can post an ad

LEO   Online?

DAN   Make a profile or something.
See?

And there's a box where you can write things.
What you're looking for.
What you're not looking for.
No smoking.
No strings attached.

No rabbits.

LEO   A stranger?

DAN   We don't have to reply.

We can put it out there

And if we get someone we don't like
We can ignore them.

Four

ANNA *and* ROBERT.

ANNA	Haven't decided who we are taking forward yet.
ROBERT	Oh.
ANNA	We're just meeting people at the moment.
ROBERT	So is this like an interview, or…?
ANNA	No, Oh no. That's very… No. More like a chat, really.
ROBERT	Okay.
ANNA	We just want to sort of see what kind of person you are. We want you Not you Whoever Maybe you To be involved
ROBERT	Involved?
ANNA	I mean, not *involved* involved
ROEBRT	What level of involved are we talking? If you need someone to pop round and play a couple of games I can do that. I can do Lego. But if it's a financial involvement
ANNA	No no
ROBERT	I'm pretty broke. That's basically why I'm here.
ANNA	We're not asking for any money. Nothing like that.
ROBERT	Okay.

ANNA   Just
             Being
             Present.
             Whenever you want to.

ROBERT   Not that big a deal, right?

             I can understand why it's a big deal for *you*, but

             I've just got to go in there.
             Do my thing.

             That's all, really (?)

ANNA   We want him or her
             them
             We want them to know about their father.
             Not just at eighteen. But throughout.

             That's the problem with the sperm bank.
             You're not allowed to know.

ROBERT   Of course

ANNA   It's all anonymous

ROBERT   Yes

ANNA   Not really how we
             'envisioned'
             Is that the right word?
             'envisioned' it.
             Not what we wanted, really.
             So we're interviewing
             Chatting
             Chatting with people
             Like this.

             It's a chat.

ROBERT   Great.

ANNA   Nicer for you.
             Can't imagine what it must be like
             Donating your...
             Your...
             Seed (?) /
             And

ROBERT   Seed?

ANNA   Then leaving and never knowing.
Walking around
Walking to the shops
Sitting on the bus and maybe
The kid sat next to you
Maybe that kid's yours.
Imagine that.

ROBERT   That doesn't bother me too much.
It's mainly the money.

ANNA   Drive myself crazy imaging that.

ROBERT   They don't give you much.
At the clinic.
For a go.
Barely covers the Uber there and back.

Bit more money if you do it privately.

ANNA   Robert, right?
Your name.

ROBERT   Yes.
Robert.

ANNA   Robert. Great. Robert.
Sorry
Double checking.
My fiancée, she does all the 'getting in contact' and stuff.
Just on her way home.

ROBERT   Okay.

ANNA   Emily. She's the one you've been speaking too.
I'm Anna.
I'm the one you'll be inseminating.

ROBERT   Yes. She said.

ANNA   We'd need you take some tests.
If that's okay.

ROBERT   Right.

ANNA	Whoever we chose. We'd need to make sure they're clear.
ROBERT	Of course.
ANNA	,
	(*To herself*.) Robert.
ROBERT	Yes?
ANNA	Oh no,
	I was just saying…
	Feeling how it sits on the tongue.
	'Robert'
	You know, Robert.
ROBERT	Right.
ANNA	We're thinking about names. For the baby.
	,
	Lovely name, yours. Robert.
ROBERT	Do you think so?
ANNA	Don't hear it very often nowadays, do you? 'Robert.'
ROBERT	Is your fiancée…?
ANNA	Any minute now, should be.
ROBERT	Great.
ANNA	Do you want some water, Rob?
ROBERT	No, thank you, I'm
ANNA	Sure?
ROBERT	Just Robert.
ANNA	Sorry?

ROBERT   I'm just Robert.
            Rob
            You said…

ANNA   For short (?)

ROBERT   Just Robert.

ANNA   Just Robert. I see I see.
            That's very respectable.

ROBERT   I think so.

ANNA   ,

            Not even your mum?

ROBERT   ?

ANNA   Does your mum call you Rob?

ROBERT   No.

ANNA   What did she call you, like, as a baby?

ROBERT   Robert.
            That's what she called me.
            When I was born
            And each time after that.

ANNA   Baby Robert?

ROBERT   Yes.

ANNA   Never really thought about a baby being called
            Robert.
            Sort of sounds like ribbit. You know. Like a frog.

ROBERT   Right.

ANNA   Not you.
            I don't mean you.
            Robert suits you.

ROBERT   Do I look like a frog?

ANNA   What I mean is
            It's a name you grow into.

            Robbie is a boy's name.
            Robert is a man.

Suits you because you're a man, you know.
You're a proper, fleshed out, real... juicy man...
man.

You know,

Fleshed out.

,

Funny imagining it the other way round.
A little baby Robert
Walking around
Oh look
It's little baby Robert
There he goes.

ROBERT   Fuck

ANNA   Little Robert with his little Robert feet and his
          little Robert water bottle.

ROBERT   Actually I'll have some water if that's

ANNA   Yes

ROBERT   Thanks

ANNA   Just going to give Emily /

ROBERT   Actually I might /

ANNA   Give her a call.

ROBERT   I might go.
          Sorry.

ANNA   What?

ROBERT   I don't know what...
          I don't normally do this kind of thing.

ANNA   No,
          It's me.
          Being weird
          Have I ballsed this up?
          I've ballsed this up, haven't I.

ROBERT   Just don't think it's for me.

ANNA   Emily will be here any minute.
            She's much better at talking to people than me.

ROBERT   I'm really sorry.

ANNA   Okay
            Look,
            Okay

            Could we just
            Have a *Men in Black* moment
            Boop.
            Erase All Memory
            And just
            Give it another go?

ROBERT   I don't know.

ANNA   Look
            It'll be easy.

            Hi.
            I'm Anna.

ROBERT   …

ANNA   This is where you say 'I'm Robert'

ROBERT   Oh.
            Er

            Hi.
            I'm Robert.

ANNA   Lovely to meet you, Robert.

            ,

            Lovely name.

Five

LEO *and* AL.

LEO	Sprinkled chocolate on top. Suddenly thought I don't know if he even wants chocolate. And I was going to come back and ask But sort of just… panicked And Sprinkled The Chocolate On
	Is that okay?
AL	Erm
LEO	I always think Fuck it. It's Chocolate. Fuck it. At the end of the day it's a bit of chocolate Who doesn't like a bit of chocolate
AL	I don't.
LEO	Oh
AL	Yeah.
LEO	Really?
AL	I love chocolate, just
LEO	On a diet?
AL	Allergic.
LEO	Fuck.
AL	Quite badly.
LEO	Sorry
AL	You didn't know
LEO	I can scrape it off.

AL	Erm
LEO	Look, Look I'll just…
	scrape
	off
	the top
	Just take the top off the / …
AL	The froth /
LEO	Just like that.
	Ta dah.
	Can't even see it now.
AL	,
	Shouldn't really risk it.
LEO	No, Obviously. Shouldn't risk it.
AL	I'm sure it's fine, but…
LEO	No, of course.
AL	Get really bad.
LEO	Really?
AL	Patches.
LEO	Patches?
AL	One time I had to go to hospital
LEO	Shit.
AL	Actually stopped breathing.
LEO	Oh my god. Oh my god are you feeling okay? Do you feel okay now?

AL	Look at you.
LEO	Do you want to go to hospital in case? I can drive you.
AL	Look at your face. Gosh you're cute.
LEO	Huh?
AL	I shouldn't be laughing. This isn't funny I'm a cunt.
LEO	So you're not…
AL	God, no. Chocolate? I'd kill myself.
LEO	Oh Oh thank God. Jesus
AL	Didn't think you'd…
LEO	For a second I thought – Jesus, For a second, thought you were about to
AL	Didn't think you'd actually scrape it off. That's golden.
LEO	It's a bit of a mess.
AL	Breathe.
LEO	Okay. I'm okay. You're okay?
AL	How much was it?
LEO	No it's
AL	No, let me pay Please If I don't pay I'm going to feel like a cunt And I'd like to avoid that.

LEO	,
	Thank you.
AL	So,
	You're 'horny human slave looking for sexy alien master'
LEO	Who?
	,
	Oh, right. Yes. That is, in fact, me, isn't it. Hello.
AL	Hi
LEO	My boyfriend wrote the ad. It's his account.
AL	Boyfriend?
LEO	He thinks he's very funny.
AL	There's two of you?
LEO	,
	Doesn't it say?
AL	Don't think so
LEO	On our profile. Pretty sure it says.
AL	Maybe I missed it.
	I mean I definitely missed it because…
LEO	Right.
AL	Boyfriend.
LEO	Is that… Does that make this difficult?
AL	It doesn't have to.
	We'd have to sort out the rules.

LEO	Rules?
AL	Set some boundaries. Just logistically What we're doing about that.
LEO	We know what we want. We know what we're looking for.
AL	Yes, Science / fiction
LEO	(*Whispering*.) Intergalactic – Sure.
AL	So I'm quite happy with that. Alien stuff
LEO	(*Whispering*.) Sure
AL	,
	Are you…
LEO	?
AL	Okay?
LEO	Just a bit…
	We're…
	A bit public.
AL	Of course. Sorry. Indoor voices.
	Didn't mean to make you feel Uncomfortable or
LEO	No no, Of course, I don't.
AL	I'm a pretty open book Woosh. I'm there.
LEO	Great.

AL   I don't do shitting.

LEO   Oh.

AL   So if that's what you're looking for

LEO   No
          God no.

AL   There's nothing wrong with it.

LEO   No,
          Of course not.
          I'm sure there's not

AL   If that is your thing
          If that is what you're into

LEO   It's not.
          Why
          Why would you say that?
          My 'thing'?

AL   Not something to be ashamed about.
          Not how I wanted to come across.

LEO   No

AL   It's just not on the cards for me.

LEO   Me neither

AL   Okay.

LEO   It's not.

AL   I believe you.

LEO   Am I giving off a vibe?

AL   A vibe?

LEO   Yes.

AL   What vibe?

LEO   I don't know.
          Like
          I want to shit on your chest
          sort of vibe.

AL   I wasn't assuming…

LEO   No

AL   Just setting boundaries.

LEO   Okay.

AL   Apart from that I'm happy with most things.

            Obviously depending on where you come
            It's going to cost you more inside the arsehole
            But anywhere else
            It's pretty much a standard rate.

LEO   Sorry?

AL   So we'd have to
            You'd have to
            Decide that
            You know
            Amongst yourselves
            Beforehand

LEO   Could you just
            Rewind that a second

AL   (*Whispering*.) *Sorry*. Indoor voices.

LEO   Cost more?

AL   In the arse.

            But I don't know if
            The alien …
            If the costume has like a flap at the back or

            Do they? Aliens.
            Have assholes?

LEO   I think there's a misunderstanding

AL   Yes, Sorry.
            I'm sure their anatomy is very different

LEO   You seem lovely

            And you know
            You're fucking gorgeous

So
There's that.

We're just…
We're not looking for…

AL   Right.

LEO   Didn't know that this would be…
            That this is a
            paid
            thing.

            We just wanted something a bit more
            Casual.

AL   I understand.

LEO   Not that I'm…
            You know,
            Not that we're against it or anything.
            Hashtag support sex-workers and that.

AL   I don't normally do this kind of thing
            I saw your guys' profile and thought it looked fun.

LEO   Sure.

AL   Got to find a way somehow.
            Rising tuition fees, student living, the whole
            rhetoric.

LEO   You're a student?

AL   Second year.
            Engineering.

LEO   Engineering. Wow. Interesting.

            ,

            That's…

AL   Aeronautical Engineering.

LEO   Oh.

            ,

Aeronautical.

,

So that's like… / spaceships?

AL   Spacecraft,

,

Yeah.

Six

EMILY *and* ANNA.

ANNA	It's called a conception cup.
EMILY	Right
ANNA	Got it from Boots.
EMILY	Looks… Fun.
ANNA	Fun?
EMILY	Interesting.
ANNA	Don't hold it like that.
EMILY	I'm not. Like what?
ANNA	Like it's a snotty tissue
EMILY	Keeping it clean. Don't want to dirty it. Fingerprints. Oils.
ANNA	Afterwards I've got to lie with my legs in the air apparently. That's what she says. On her blog.
EMILY	She's very…
ANNA	Really / good.
EMILY	Descriptive.
ANNA	There's more if you / scroll down.
EMILY	Oh look. There's a photo. She's included a photo.
ANNA	If you scroll past that. There's a bit For partners.
EMILY	A lot of photos. Quite intense.

ANNA   Most of it will drip out,
            That's what she says,

EMILY   Right.

ANNA   When I'm ready to stand up.

EMILY   So I've got to insert this / thingy, this...

ANNA   'Insert'?

EMILY   Conception cup,
            Into you,
            And then I can pour it into the top
            And then we wait?

ANNA   I can pour it.

EMILY   You'll be on your back.

ANNA   Afterwards, yes.

EMILY   So shall I... hold it?
            Whilst you pour?

ANNA   That's okay.
            I know it makes you uncomfortable.

EMILY   I never said that.

ANNA   You just seem –

EMILY   I am very comfortable.

ANNA   Okay.

EMILY   ,

            Am I making *you* uncomfortable?

ANNA   It's started getting a bit...

EMILY   A bit...?

ANNA   Well, a bit...
            Clinical

EMILY   Clinical?

ANNA   'Insert'

EMILY   Sorry.

ANNA   Not a bad thing.
                But if you don't know what to do,
                If you don't know how to feel,
                You don't have to pretend.
                It's okay.

EMILY   I want to be here.
                I want to be with you
                Be part of it.

ANNA   You are, you're part of it
                You're part of so much of it.
                You will be.
                The birth.
                The coming home from the hospital.
                The first steps. First words.
                You're going to be part of all that.

                But
                I'm quite happy doing just this bit just me.

EMILY   ,

                So, you want me to just…

                ,

                Watch?

                ,

                Like sit on the side and watch you?

ANNA   Well, no,
                That's a bit creepy

EMILY   God, I feel like a man.
                Is that what I am?
                Am I a dad from the eighties?

ANNA   Stop it.

EMILY   I am
                I'm an eighties dad.

ANNA   Don't make me laugh
                I can't laugh with this in.
                It'll shoot back out

EMILY   No thank you.

ANNA   I'll come get you
             Once I'm done.

             Okay?

Seven

LEO *and* AL.

LEO	Got his arm up You know Like he's a flying. Like he's a superhero.
AL	He'll be dreaming.
LEO	Does it all the time. With his fist You know, like Arm out, with the fist.
AL	Yes.
LEO	You can have a look If you like
AL	No, no Let him sleep
LEO	Pop your head round the door
AL	Best not to, Just in case Best not to wake him.
LEO	You're fine. He'll sleep through anything.
AL	Wouldn't want to ruin the dream.
LEO	Sometime I think I could be, You know, Murdered Actually being mutilated And he'll sleep through it. Worst superhero ever.
AL	Right.
	,
LEO	You can use any of those.
AL	Oh.

LEO	They're all clean in that pile, so
	,
	Except the purple one That's mine.
AL	Right.
LEO	Not *mine*. That sounded a bit… It's not *my towel*. I'm not possessive. Just like using the purple one.
AL	Right.
LEO	Soft.
AL	Sure
LEO	You can use that one. If you want. There are other colours
AL	Was about to head off actually. Trying not to wake you.
LEO	No no, You didn't I was already awake. Would've waited anyway So by all means, If you fancy it
AL	That's okay.
LEO	Okay.
AL	,
	Unless you want me to take a shower with you. If that's what you're asking.
LEO	Just meant It can get quite sweaty In the costume Just thought you might fancy one

	On your own
	Before you leave.
AL	If you'd like to watch
	If that's something you'd like
	Won't cost any more

LEO   (*Whispering*.) Oooh
       Oops.
       Ummm
       Sorry
       Bit loud.

       Don't want to wake Superman.

AL   (*Whispering*.) Sorry. Indoor voices.

LEO   Actually I'm
       I'm not saying anything to him.
       About the money.
       So

       If you could just, erm,
       If we can keep it like that.

AL   Between us.

LEO   Don't think he would really understand.

AL   You can pay in cash
       Next time
       If that's easier
       Harder to trace.

LEO   Next time?

AL   Oh.

       If there was something that wasn't...

LEO   No.
       Fuck.
       No no

AL   If it wasn't working
       If it

LEO   No,
       It did.

It definitely did.
Did you think so?

AL   I had fun.

LEO   Me too.

AL   You both seemed into it.

LEO   I was.
I was, really

And he was,
You know

I was worried because
Really this was my idea
But he was definitely...
I mean,
When you've been together as long as we have
I'd like to think I can tell when he's...
You know
And when he's not.
And he definitely was.

AL   Great.

LEO   I just
I reckon it might just be a one-time thing.

AL   I understand.

LEO   You know,
Like
I had this
We had this thing
That we wanted to do
And we did it
Box ticked.

Eight

ANNA *and* ROBERT.

ANNA   ,

                 Everything
                 okay?

                 ,

                 Robert?

                                    ROBERT   Yes
                                                  I'm just –

                 Sorry
                 Making sure
                 you're
                 okay in there.

                 ,

                 Did you find it?

                 The lube
                 Can you see it?

                 ,

                 In the basket by
                 the sink.

                                                  Yes, got it.

                 Good.
                 Good.

                 ,

                 Would you like
                 some music?

                                                  What?

                 If you feel like
                 that would help.

                                                  Could you
                                                  just…

Whatever's
comfortable.

                    Bit off-putting.
                    Can't really…
                    Whilst
Oh.   you're…
Yes.
Sorry.

                    Keep losing my
                    erection.
                    Trying to stay
                    in the mood.
Of course.

                    I'll let you
                    know when
No, no
obviously.

,

If there's
anything you
need
you just let me
know.

,

There's a candle
If that helps?

ROBERT   All done.

ANNA   Great.
            Wow.
            Fast.

ROBERT   Left it in there.
            On top of the toilet.
            Ready for you to…

ANNA   Thanks for doing this again.

ROBERT	No problem.
ANNA	Obviously it's quite expected
ROBERT	Sure
ANNA	To need to try a couple of times before it Before it sort of sticks (?) or whatever it does.
ROBERT	I don't mind. I'm very happy to.
ANNA	Thank you.
ROBERT	As many times as it takes.
ANNA	Not too many, I hope.
ROBERT	No.
	' Is Emily…?
ANNA	At work.
ROBERT	Back soon or?
ANNA	Academic conference. Late night for Emily.
ROBERT	Right.
ANNA	Probably best. Keep her busy. She's not very good with this side of things. She'll make a great mum once it's all done.
ROBERT	Of course.
ANNA	Should probably do my part now. Whilst everything is… fresh.
ROBERT	Can I stay?
ANNA	It's very boring. Lying on my back.

Legs in the air.
Nothing much to see, really.

ROBERT   Stay here
          As in,
          For a bit?

          ,

          As in...

          ,

          Just for the short term.

ANNA   Sorry
          Are you asking to move in?

ROBERT   Is that a bit forward?

          I wasn't really sure how to ask.

          I was hoping to ask when Emily was here, but,

ANNA   Move in with me and Emily?

ROBERT   I'm very clean.
          I don't smoke.

ANNA   God.

ROBERT   They're increasing my rent.
          Can't afford it.
          Even with the extra cash from this.
          Student loan only gets you so far.

          I noticed your spare room.

ANNA   The baby's room?

ROBER   I'll be gone by then.
          Just somewhere for a few days
          Maybe a month.
          Time to sort myself out

ANNA   Right.

ROBERT   And I'll be here to help.
          With...

We can do
'This'
As much as you need.

ANNA   Listen, Robert.

We really appreciate all your help.
Everything you're doing to help us.
We're very grateful.

But living here?

I don't think that's going to work.

I'm sorry.

ROBERT   I understand.

ANNA   I can ask around, if you like.
I'm sure we'll know someone.

ROBERT   Thank you.

ANNA   When do you need somewhere by?

ROBERT   ,

Tomorrow.

ANNA   Oh.

,

ROBERT   It's late. I know.
I only had the idea now
In there
Whilst I was…

Popped into my head.
Mid-way.
Thinking
This is a nice bathroom.
I would be quite happy if this was my bathroom.

ANNA   Do you not have anyone you can stay with?
Any family?

ROBERT   …

ANNA   ,

              Fuck.
              Okay, erm

              ,

              I'd have to talk to Emily.

ROBERT   Of course
              Yes, obviously.

              ,

              And if she's okay with it?

ANNA   I don't know.

              I'd really need to talk to Emily first.

Nine

LEO *and* DAN.

DAN	If you wanted to do it again
LEO	Sorry?
DAN	Hypothetically If you wanted to.
LEO	Do you? Want to? Again.
DAN	I'm just talking hypothetically
LEO	Thought it was a one-time thing. Box ticked.
DAN	Me too.
LEO	A two-time thing?
DAN	If you wanted to. Or Something more regular, maybe. , We don't have to
LEO	No, no I do I want I'm Glad.
DAN	Smiling.
LEO	Happy that you…
DAN	I love that smile.
LEO	You looked like you… [enjoyed]
DAN	I did.
LEO	You see what I mean? About 'The Approach'.

      He's just really got it.
      He wasn't trying to be too…
      Oooooo
      Look at me.
      I'm green.

      He was
      just
      very

DAN   Yes.

LEO   Intelligent.

DAN   I think he liked it.

LEO   So like,
      A regular thing?
      Like a regular Wednesday thing?

DAN   Doesn't have to be Wednesday.

LEO   No, of course.
      Just

DAN   Hypothetically.

LEO   Hypothetical Wednesdays.

DAN   Might not want to.
      Might have thought we were really fucking odd.

LEO   Do you think?

DAN   Blocked our number.
      Covered himself in tomato soup in the shower.

LEO   Was I too much?
      Was it the music?
      Do you think the music was too much?

DAN   Like with skunks.
      Removing the smell.

LEO   Skunks?

DAN   You know,
      In films.

LEO	…
DAN	It's a joke
LEO	Did I smell?
DAN	I'm joking. You smell great.
LEO	It's an expensive Jo Malone.
DAN	You smelt sexy.
LEO	, You think?
DAN	Very.
LEO	Okay. Okay cool. , I'll ask him. See when he's free. If he's free on Wednesdays.

Ten

ANNA *and* EMILY.

EMILY   Put him in the spare room for a few days
             Give him / time.

ANNA   A few *days*?

EMILY   Can't leave him on the streets
             Is that what you want / to do?

ANNA   Bit of an / exaggeration.

EMILY   Have him sleep in his car?

ANNA   Don't get me wrong
             I like the boy.
             He's interesting
             In his own way

EMILY   (*Whispering*.) He can hear you.

ANNA   He's going to be the father of our child.
             There's got to be some boundaries.

             I'm not sure I feel comfortable living with the
             father of my child.

EMILY   Okay so
             Let's
             Treat it like a trial period.

ANNA   A 'trial period'?

EMILY   See how it goes.

ANNA   We're putting him up, not employing him.

EMILY   You know what I'm saying.

ANNA   A trial period
             Sounds very…

EMILY   Not to his face
             Won't tell him that.

ANNA   Capitalist.

EMILY   See how he gets on.
          See how it works
          Him living here.

ANNA   Longer?

EMILY   See how it goes.

ANNA   Thought you said a few days.

EMILY   Just until the baby comes.
          You know what work's like.
          It's a lot of late nights for me at the moment.
          Might be nice to have someone here.
          Help sort things out.

ANNA   I'm fine.
          We're fine.

EMILY   Okay, if it doesn't work then…

          Right now, it's just a trial.

          Okay?

Eleven

DAN *and* AL.

DAN	Should be here any minute.
AL	If Wednesday isn't a good day…?
DAN	He's just in traffic.
AL	We can always change days.
DAN	Told him not to take the car. I cycle in most days. Avoid the traffic.
AL	Cyclist.
DAN	Wouldn't go that far.
AL	Cyclist legs.
DAN	, Do you think?
AL	They're nice.
DAN	Joined the environmental committee at sixth form to help my UCAS. Something extra-curricular Ended up cycling to save the world.
AL	Does Leo cycle?
DAN	Don't tell him I told you, [but…] He's scared of bicycles. Never took the stabilisers off. It's adorable really. , Can I get you anything? Shouldn't be long now.
AL	Did you like school?
DAN	Got on with it, I suppose. Like everyone else.

AL   You seem like the kind of person that did well at
            school.

            Academic.

DAN   Oh no.
            I was very average.
            Nothing special.

            Not like you
            Mr Aeronautical Engineer

AL   Mechanical.

DAN   What's that?

AL   I study mechanical engineering.

DAN   Oh.
            Sorry.
            I thought you did Aeronautical.

AL   That's okay.
            Easy mistake to make.
            They're all the same really.

DAN   What's that then?
            Mechanical?

AL   Whole bunch of things.

            Fridges. Gas turbines. Lifts. Escalators.

            ,

            Bicycles.

DAN   Really?

AL   ,

            Are you satisfied?

DAN   ?

AL   With our arrangement.

DAN   You're very good at…
            I think you're great at what Leo wants.

AL	What about you? What do you want?
DAN	I normally come when he comes. I get off on him.
	It's his thing really. This.
AL	What's your thing?
DAN	As in…
	In the bedroom?
AL	Scenarios.
DAN	Don't think I have a 'thing'.
AL	Try me.
DAN	I'm vanilla. Honest. Nothing special.
AL	I won't laugh.
DAN	Wish I was more exciting.
	,
	I mean…
	,
	No.
AL	There. There it was.
DAN	No no.
AL	There's something there. I saw it. Just then. You stopped yourself.
	Go on.
DAN	,
	In school,
	The boys' changing room had this shower room.
	A wall with shower heads, in a row.

After PE, we'd all get in.

All the boys in this one room together.

Ahh this is bad
Sounds so cliché
Feel like…
A bad gay

,

Some of them would hurry to get dressed,
Or just not be thinking about it
Just talking and drying and changing
And they'd put their boxers back on before they
had dried themselves…
Their bodies still wet
And so
The boxers
They'd soak through quite quickly
And you could just see the outline

I always thought that was quite…

I think about that sometimes.

,

AL   I've still got my football kit from school.
Bit mucky but

I can bring it next week if you'd like?

Would you like that?

Twelve

ROBERT *and* ANNA.

ROBERT   It's a pressure fit gate.

            No screws or anything
            Comes off whenever you want.
            Can untighten it here
            Same on the other side.

ANNA   Right.

ROBERT   You want them so the gate opens like this, away
            from the door.

            Put it on the other way round first
            Kept bashing against it.

            We'll have to buy the extension kit for the back
            door because it's wider than eighty centimetres.
            Anything wider than eighty centimetres you'll
            need the extension kit

ANNA   Great, that's

ROBERT   On sale at John Lewis.
            I can get some more
            Put them on the doors upstairs if you like.

ANNA   This is great
            Really
            Thank you
            But…

            It's a bit early.
            Don't you think?

ROBERT   Not really.

ANNA   I'm not even pregnant yet.
            Don't want to jinx anything.

ROBERT   It'll happen before you know it
            Suddenly there'll be a little thing
            Crawling and walking all over the place

ANNA   I suppose

ROBERT   I didn't think I was going to be that fussed really.
           No offence.

           Now it's like…
           I'm going to have a baby in the world.
           Fuck. You know?

ANNA   Yes.

ROBERT   Everything feels a bit different.

           I've started having dreams. Is that weird?
           Having this dream that the baby keeps falling
           down the stairs
           Crawling out of that room
           On repeat.

           Woke up this morning and went to John Lewis
           and bought one of these.

           Make sure it's all safe.

ANNA   Great.
           That's great.
           And thank you, honestly Robert, thank you.
           And this is your house too
           We want you to feel like it's somewhere you
           can live.
           Happily.

           But also,
           It's our house.
           Do you see?

           Emily and I
           We've got a plan. How we want things to be.
           Once the baby comes

           Maybe next time
           Run it by us.
           Before you… you know. Gates.

ROBERT   Emily's suggested it.

ANNA   ,

           Oh.

ROBERT   Told her about the dream.
           Last night.
           When she came home from work
           We had a few beers in the lounge.

           You'd already fallen asleep.

           She mentioned getting some gates.

           I thought I'd…
           Out my own pocket.
           A little thank you.

ANNA   Right.

           Well,
           Thank you.

ROBERT   Talked about some ideas I had for painting my
           room.
           For the baby.

ANNA   Painting?

ROBERT   Got some samples from B&Q. Tried them out on
           the wall over here.

           See?

           Emily thinks number two or three.

           What do you think?

ANNA   Erm
           Sorry
           Is that to paint the whole room?

ROBERT   Got some time on Friday.
           Hopefully get it done then.

           Have a sit with them.
           Let me know.

           ,

           We're leaning more towards number two at the
           moment.

Thirteen

LEO *and* DAN.

LEO	Twitter's popping off.
DAN	They're impressive, I'll give you that.
LEO	The photos aren't very good Just people driving past in their cars But you can sort of make it out.
DAN	Looks like there's quite a few
LEO	Three. Surely you can't make three in one night So that pretty much debunks / any
DAN	It could have been a group.
LEO	What?
DAN	Nothing. Would make sense if it was a group. Not just one bloke on his own in the middle of the night with a lawnmower.
LEO	Seem legit Look identical to the ones in Hull a couple months ago. Who's travelling down from Hull to hoax a crop circle? See Look at that.
DAN	I guess.
LEO	Should drive down before it gets dark.
DAN	Tonight?
LEO	Get some great shots on your camera. Way better than these.
DAN	Not tonight.
LEO	What?
DAN	He'll be here any minute.

LEO	Tell him we forgot.
DAN	It's Wednesday. It's always Wednesday.
LEO	He'll understand
DAN	Can't just cancel ten minutes before. He comes from Luton.
LEO	You know where he lives?
DAN	He told me he's started cycling in.
LEO	From Luton?
DAN	Don't want to let him down. It's rude. Especially for something that's not...
LEO	What?
DAN	Probably not real.
LEO	You don't think it's real?
DAN	I don't know. Do you?
LEO	I haven't seen it yet.
DAN	There'll be more next week.
LEO	Not like this.
DAN	I don't feel good about fucking him off to drive eighty miles into the middle of God knows where to take a picture of a circle in a field because someone on Twitter says so. I'm sorry. I think that's fair.
LEO	, Okay. ,
DAN	Sorry if that...
LEO	I'm not really... 'in the mood' anyway.

DAN   Didn't mean to upset you.

LEO   Don't fancy having sex right now.

DAN   No, okay.

LEO   Thinking I'll run a bath.

DAN   I feel bad.

LEO   Don't.

DAN   ,

            I don't want to stop you.

            ,

            You go and see the crop circle.

            I'll stay here and wait for Al.

            ,

            You can still take my camera if you like?
            It's in my top drawer in the bedroom.

Fourteen

ANNA *and* EMILY.

EMILY   With the treatment there's a better chance it'll
            happen.
            That's what the doctor said.

ANNA   It won't.

EMILY   Said we can keep trying.

ANNA   She said it won't.
            That's what she was saying, really.
            Couldn't you hear it?

            Was listening to her and
            Felt like
            Failing
            Letting us down

EMILY   No

ANNA   Keep thinking
            That if I couldn't do this,

EMILY   Hey hey hey
            Deep breaths.

ANNA   No, I'm

EMILY   Come on, deep breath.

            ,

            That's it.
            Another one.

            ,

            Good.

            ,

            If you want to keep trying…
            We can. I'm happy.

ANNA   Should still talk about it

EMILY   As long as it takes.

ANNA   Because it probably won't happen.
            Even if we keep trying / even if we...

EMILY   We don't know that.

ANNA   Okay.
            But,
            We do.

            We know.

EMILY   Anna

ANNA   No,
            No 'Anna'.
            No saying my name
            This is important.
            Because there's a lot of pressure on me if we
            don't talk about this.

EMILY   Okay.

ANNA   If we're going to keep throwing money at this.
            It's important to keep in mind that there are no
            guarantees.

            And if it doesn't work,
            The treatment,
            Where we go from there.

EMILY   ,

            There are other options, yes?

            ,

            We could adopt.

ANNA   No.

            ,

            Sorry I know you shouldn't say that. I know that
            makes me sound like an awful human being but
            I just
            don't want
            To do that.

            That's not how I wanted it.

EMILY   Okay.

         ,

         I could try.

ANNA   ,

EMILY   If we wanted to.

ANNA   You'd hate it.

EMILY   Just an idea.

ANNA   You hate maternity clothes.

EMILY   Not 'hate', just

ANNA   You think they're ugly and unflattering
         Which I always thought was a bit sexist actually
         but

EMILY   They are

ANNA   Of course they are
         But you don't say that out loud.

         And you don't like scans

EMILY   No.

ANNA   You think the jelly's too cold and reminds you of
         when you had a hernia.

EMILY   It does.

ANNA   You never wanted to carry.
         Every time we talk you say you can never see
         yourself…

EMILY   I didn't.

         But I talked to Robert / and –

ANNA   Robert?

EMILY   He suggested that
         Maybe
         If we wanted to …
         You know,

Biologically,
Then maybe it's our next best option.

ANNA   You told Robert?

EMILY   He's got to know.
            He's part of this.

ANNA   He suggested this then? Robert.

EMILY   He was very understanding.

ANNA   Great.

EMILY   And watching you both do it these past months
            It doesn't seem so scary any more.

            I know it's not how you planned it
            But if it means we get the nine months.
            We get the showers and the morning sickness and
            the hospital visits and the birth and the building it
            all together.

            And if you can't do it,
            At least you can be near it.

Fifteen

LEO *and* DAN.

LEO	I fucked Ryan.
DAN	,
LEO	Thought it would be best if I just came out with it Because I regret it. I do Of course. And
DAN	When?
LEO	Sorry?
DAN	When did you.
LEO	When? Erm, Yesterday. It's been eating away at me Eating Ever since Ever since we… I'm coming to you I'm here now I'm telling you straight away. Thought it would be better like this Straight away If I came to you. I can't keep things. Never been able to. Not that kind of person. Can't cover up things. Fucking hate it Fucking hate the *pretending*
DAN	I went to work today.
LEO	, Yes

DAN   I had a meeting.
        With Ryan.
        This morning.

        We talked.
        I made a joke.
        Before we went in I made a joke about the water
        cooler.

        He laughed.

        ,

        Do you know how stupid that makes me feel?

LEO   I wanted to tell you sooner.

DAN   Laughing at my joke.

        Probably thinking poor guy
        Not a fucking clue I've shagged his boyfriend
        I should probably laugh at his joke now.
        Throw a dog a bone.

LEO   He wouldn't have thought that.

DAN   Laughing.
        Like an idiot.

LEO   He's very professional.

DAN   Fucking hell.

LEO   My palms are sweating.
        Could you just
        Okay
        I'd just like to say what I need to say because
        Well,
        I've thought this through a lot
        How I want to say things
        And everything's just slipping away right now
        Slipping out my brain
        Please, / let me

DAN   Come on, then.

LEO   You got close with Al.
        I see it. Between you.
        Felt

	Removed Wanted you to feel it too, I guess.
DAN	Jealous.
LEO	Maybe. Yes.
DAN	Why didn't you say?
LEO	I don't know.
DAN	You need something You feel something You say it. You say it with your mouth Moving your mouth Like this Moving your tongue like LA LA LA LA LA LA Saying it. See? Like that. Communicate.
LEO	I know.
DAN	Not fuck someone else.
LEO	I know.
DAN	Is this a game? Are you playing a game?
LEO	No. No of course / I'm not.
DAN	Toxic fucking games 'wanted you to feel it too' What even is that?
LEO	Lately it's been Feels like A lot of space Here Between us. And I just don't know how to close it.
DAN	He was your idea.

LEO   No, I know, I

DAN   It's your role-play
           It's your choice
           It's your game
           Can't keep making up new rules then breaking
           them.

LEO   I'm ready to stop.

DAN   I don't want this.
           I don't want to play this game.

LEO   Yes yes yes
           Okay good
           Because that's what I want.
           No more games.
           We can just
           Shut it all down
           And I know that doesn't make this any better
           And I know I should have just come to you and
           talked to you about this rather than / hurting you

DAN   Fucking someone else.

LEO   And I'm sorry and I feel disgusting and I want to
           be with you
           And I think if we keep with the way things are
           then I might do it again.

           ,

           I just

           I think stopping this with Al
           Taking a breath.
           I think that's going to really help.

           I know it's my thing.
           I'll sort it.
           I'll tell him we're not…
           Any more.

DAN   ,

           I don't want to do that.

LEO   What?

DAN   He likes me.

LEO   No he doesn't

DAN   We have a good time.

LEO   Dan.

DAN   He's interested in the things I'm interested in.

LEO   We pay him, Dan.
        That's why he likes us.
        We're paying him.

        ,

        He comes here because he's paid
        Usually by the hour usually
        Sometimes a set fee for the evening.

        It's a service.

        ,

        I didn't tell you / because –

DAN   I think you should go.

LEO   ,

        I'm telling you
        I'm being honest with you.

DAN   I want you out.

LEO   No.

        Let's talk.
        Figure it out.

DAN   I don't want that now.

        Get out.

LEO   ,

        I live here.

        ,

        I live here, Dan.

        Where do you want me to go?

Sixteen

ANNA *and* EMILY.

EMILY	A lot of bleeding Didn't know what was happening.
ANNA	Came straight from work.
EMILY	They did a scan.
ANNA	Okay, good, okay. Good they did a scan.
EMILY	Apparently quite normal Lots of women bleed at some point during pregnancy. That's what she said, the doctor.
ANNA	No phone this week. The / conference.
EMILY	I know, conference.
ANNA	Can't have my phone on.
EMILY	No.
ANNA	Should be there for you. Kept thinking about how scared you'd be All on your own.
EMILY	Well, Not on my own. Robert came.
ANNA	, Right
EMILY	He was in his… working, In his room Needed someone. He had his car
ANNA	Me and you, should've been

EMILY	He drove me there Waited
ANNA	Don't know anything about him, not really.
EMILY	Sat in the car for hours Just to drive me back.
ANNA	Where is he from? Do you know where he's from?
EMILY	Anna
ANNA	London? Doncaster? The moon? Has he got any friends? Family? Where are all his friends and family? Can you answer any of that? A total fucking stranger Living here, living in our flat.
EMILY	Did you want me to go alone? Would you have felt better?
ANNA	Maybe. Yes. In some fucked way yes maybe yes I think I would have. ' Sorry, I'm…
EMILY	Can't you be happy someone was there? He's been good. Supportive and understanding, and –
ANNA	Going to take some time off. After the conference, I think. Be here. If you need me.
EMILY	You're being silly.
ANNA	I want to.
EMILY	We need the money Everything we can get now.

ANNA   Okay,
              Well,
              I'll figure something out.
              Work from home.
              If they'll let me.

EMILY   Don't need to.

ANNA   I want to.

EMILY   Okay.

              I'd like that.

ANNA   Good.
              Me too.

              Come here.

              ,

              Will put in a request in the morning.

EMILY   Might want to ask Robert first.
              Just make sure.

ANNA   ,

              What?

EMILY   His university degree.
              Most of it's online now.

              Might be a bit tight.
              Wi-Fi bandwidth and all that.

              Just good to double check.

Seventeen

LEO *and* AL.

AL	How have you been?
	My nipples are out Sorry, Was just in the shower. Heard the doorbell and wrapped this round me. Hope you don't mind.
LEO	Why are you here?
AL	Bit abrupt.
LEO	Sorry I just Er
	Wasn't expecting to…
	Didn't know you would…
	Why are you / here?
AL	Is everything okay, Leo?
LEO	(*Shouting.*) Dan!
	(*To* AL.) Can you just get Dan, please.
AL	I don't think he wants to speak to you.
LEO	(*Shouting.*) It's Leo!
	(*To* AL.) We spoke on WhatsApp.
	(*Shouting.*) Dan, are you there?!
AL	Can't hear you from the shower. He's just jumped in. Likes to watch me shower first, Get himself off, Watch me shower and then After he comes He'll get in the shower and clean himself. You know what he's like.

,

Maybe you don't.

,

You never really knew what he liked.

LEO	Can I come in?
AL	I don't think that's a good idea.
LEO	Okay, Well.

I think that's a bit...

AL	?
LEO	It's not your flat.
AL	Here to pick up some last bits, yes?
LEO	Territorial.
AL	Hold on.

AL *disappears*.

LEO   Don't think you're entitled to –

Excuse me.

Hello?

Sorry but you can't just

Can you open the door, please?

Hello?

Dan?

Can you hear me?

AL *reappears*.

AL   Sorry.

We get a horrible draught if we keep the door open.
Is it just the one box?

Careful. It's heavy.
Your slow cooker is at the bottom.

	Is it all there? Can check if there's anything else?
LEO	He kicked me out because of you.

,

Because he found out.

AL	That's really nothing to do / with me.
LEO	I told him About our Financial Arrangement.

I was so scared of losing him that I kept this thing
This secret
I kept it
So that I wouldn't
And then
I lost him anyway.

AL	I don't know why you're telling me this.
LEO	And he made me feel bad. He made me feel really bad And rightly I felt Horrendous

Look.

I'm even still fucking…
Blocked nose,
When I talk about it.

Anyway.
Not now.
Because
Flash fucking forward
Here you are.

AL	Leo
LEO	With him. You. The atomic bomb.

	Paying for the grenade that blew us to pieces. So I think I deserve some… Spending all that time feeling shitty about myself And really He's just as bad now Isn't he.
AL	You should go.
LEO	I think I'll just stay here And I'll wait, actually.
AL	Leo.
LEO	How much more time have you got left? What has he paid for? An hour? Two? The whole evening. I'll wait here. Until your time is up.
AL	Dan's not paying.
LEO	, What?
AL	It's not an arrangement Any more. I live here. With Dan. Together.
LEO	,
AL	…
LEO	,
AL	I'm sure we'll be in touch Over WhatsApp If we find anything else.
LEO	, Purple towel. , That's my towel.

AL   Oh. This?

            We share all the towels between us now.

            Dan isn't precious about whose towel is whose.

LEO   That one is mine.
            The purple one.

            ,

            I'd like it.

            ,

            I'd like to take that towel with me.

AL   You're making this harder than it needs to be.
            I don't think you really want that.
            Not really.

LEO   ,

            I really want my towel.

AL   ,

            Okay.

,

            Shall I put it the box?

            There you go.

            ,

            Happy?

            ,

            Is there anything else, Leo?

            We get a horrible draught if we keep the door open.

Eighteen

ANNA *and* ROBERT.

ANNA	Don't expect you to move out straight away. Give you some time, of course To the end of the week. Find somewhere new.
ROBERT	Oh.
ANNA	Might be a bit tight. Wi-Fi bandwidth and all that Once I start working for home
ROBERT	Baby isn't due for a couple months.
ANNA	We're ordering bits and bobs Cot, pushchair, et cetera. All arriving soon. Will be good, having some space.
ROBERT	Where?
ANNA	Sorry?
ROBERT	I don't have anywhere to go.
ANNA	Been having a look Just a gander What's on the market. Got a list of places that might work. Hopefully give you a head start.
ROBERT	Does Emily know about this?
ANNA	And most of your course is online now Isn't it? So you don't even need to be in the city.
ROBERT	She didn't say anything last night. Had a couple of beers on the sofa.
ANNA	Might find somewhere cheaper if you moved out a little further Might be better for you to move away.
ROBERT	, I'm not sure I want to do that.

ANNA   ,

Sorry?

ROBERT   I'm quite settled now.

ANNA   You'll move anyway
When the baby comes.
Now just a couple months earlier.

ROBERT   I assumed we would repurpose your office space.
Put the baby in there.

ANNA   What?

ROBERT   Think I'll stay in my room.
Quite like it now that it's painted.

ANNA   It's not...
You don't pay for...
We let you live here.

ROBERT   A mutually beneficial arrangement
Works for everyone.

ANNA   Not me.

Doesn't work for me.

ROBERT   ,

It works for Emily.

ANNA   Want you to leave.

ROBERT   Wouldn't want to put Emily in the middle.

ANNA   Calling her.

ROBERT   I don't think so.

ANNA   Hear what she says.

ROBERT   You can try if you like.

Won't pick up.

ANNA   ,

What?

ROBERT   Won't have any signal.

On the Tube.

She'll be on the Tube now.

,

Every day at this time she's on the Tube.
Finishes work about…
Ten minutes ago
And now,
For the next twenty-seven minutes,
She's on the Tube.

Did you know that?

,

I live in your house
I eat your food
Your fiancée is carrying my baby.

,

I think it's best to forget this conversation.
Keep our arrangement as it is.
Don't you?

Maybe we should
Have a *Men in Black* moment
Boop.
Erase All Memory
And
Forget all about this.

,

Okay?

Shall we do that?

,

Yes. I think so.

,

Great.

I'll talk to Emily about repurposing the office.

She'll be off the Tube soon.

Nineteen

LEO *and* DAN.

DAN	Cappuccino Chocolate on top
LEO	You remember.
DAN	How's it all / going?
LEO	Really well. Really well thanks.
DAN	You still with Ryan?
LEO	'With'? We were never 'With'
DAN	Oh. , Sorry.
LEO	No, I don't think that's… We never wanted… It was always meant to be a casual thing.
DAN	Right.
LEO	Short term Every now and then That sort of thing. Couldn't see it working long term. He's into some weird stuff. Not for me. , What about you? With / [you know]
DAN	Heard you moved back in with your mum?
LEO	Where did you hear that?

DAN   Nowhere.
        Just
        The office.

LEO   Is that going round the office?

DAN   Wouldn't read much into it.
        You know how it is.

LEO   Who in the office?

DAN   I don't have very long.

LEO   Was it Jane?

DAN   Jane?

LEO   Dyed her hair pink.
        Just the top bit.

DAN   Leo.

LEO   Like an iced gem.

DAN   I'm leaving.

LEO   ,

        Oh.

        Congratulations (?)

        Didn't know you'd applied for something.

DAN   Not the job.
        I am leaving the job but
        Because
        I'm *leaving* leaving.

        ,

        He wants to be closer to home.
        His home.
        Got a job near.
        We've decided to move up
        Together.
        I want to go too.

        We're moving in with his folks for a bit.
        Get our own place eventually.

LEO   Why are you telling me this?

DAN   I thought
           If you're still living with your mum
           You might want to stay in the flat?

           Not for free.
           I'd rent it to you. Cheaply.

LEO   Rent it to me?

DAN   A bit cheaper than if it was someone else.

LEO   Rent me my own flat?

DAN   I'm trying to be nice

LEO   Yeah, well
           Thank you, but
           No.
           Thank you.

DAN   Okay.

           ,

           Just thought.

LEO   ,

           I actually…

           There was a part of my brain that convinced itself
           you'd invited me here because

           That you were going to ask if I wanted

           Me and you.

           Again.

           Give it a go.

DAN   ,

           Sorry.

LEO   When do you leave?

DAN   Today.

LEO   Right. Wow.

DAN   He's picking me up here.

LEO   What about work?

DAN   Gave my notice last month.

LEO   Have you found something?

DAN   Going to land and then just... see what's out
           there, I guess.

LEO   You don't have a job?

DAN   I have thought about this actually.

LEO   Leaving your flat
           Leaving your job for someone you've known half
           a minute.

DAN   Over a year now.

LEO   It's quite a lot for him to expect you to do that.

DAN   It was a mutual decision.

LEO   Won't walk into another one
           At your level
           Not with how things are at the moment.

DAN   I think I'm only still at this job because it worked
           for us.

           ,

           Ready for something new.

           Think I've been ready for a while.

LEO   ,

           Is it better?
           With him?

           ,

           No sorry don't answer that.

           ,

DAN   He listens to me.

             When we talk.
             When we're at dinner.
             When we watch a film.

LEO   Yes.

             ,

             Cute.
             Happy for you.

             ,

DAN   Let me know if you change your mind about the
             flat.

             A moment.

             Then,
             A spaceship lands.

             DAN *puts on a space helmet, gets in, and flies*
             away.

             LEO *watches him disappear into space.*

Twenty

ANNA, EMILY, *and* ROBERT.

EMILY   Can someone turn out the lights?

ANNA   He'll start crying
         God
         Don't

EMILY   He'll be fine.

ROBERT   The lighter isn't…
         Ah.
         Here we go.

EMILY   Do you want me to /

ROBERT   Got it now.

ANNA   He's in the cot.

ROBERT   Is he asleep?
         Think / he's asleep.

EMILY   Probably /

ANNA   He's always asleep /

ROBERT   I'll get his bib

ANNA   He hasn't tried cake before.

ROBERT   Are we ready?

EMILY   One sec.
         Have you got the camera?

ANNA   This is big. Is it a tray bake?

ROBERT   It's flickering. Don't want the candle to

EMILY   Cover it with you hand.

ANNA   You bought a one-year-old a tray bake?
         How are we going to eat this?

ROBERT   There's a breeze.
         It keeps flickering.

EMILY   Ready?

ROBERT   Here.

EMILY   (*Starting to sing 'Happy Birthday'.*)
                Haaaaa…

                Guys!

                ROBERT *joins in.*

                ANNA *doesn't.*

EMILY/ROBERT
                Happy birthday to you
                Happy birthday to you
                Happy birthday baby Robert
                Happy birthday to you.

                They blow out the candle.

                Darkness.

                ANNA, *watching the baby.*

                A moment.

                Then,
                A small, green ALIEN *levitates out of the cot.*

                Mid-air, it turns to face ANNA.

                The ALIEN *smiles at her.*

                End.

www.nickhernbooks.co.uk

facebook.com/nickhernbooks

twitter.com/nickhernbooks